Traditionally, this is the place in t[]
personalities, and friends of the []
we certainly appreciate kind wo[]
book needed something different. So, instead, we chose to endorse
the work of innovative, hard-working young leaders out there who
are making the world a better place. Please take a moment to be
inspired by the incredible things that these kids are doing!

—ADAM & TODD

Shea Smith, 16—Missouri: Shea was diagnosed with scoliosis at age
eleven. The condition, an abnormal curvature of the spine, can cause
chronic back pain, disfigurement, and heart and lung problems. Since
her diagnosis, she has become an advocate for kids dealing with the
condition. She created a campaign called Catching the Curve to raise
awareness of scoliosis and help provide support for kids suffering with
it. Shea published a book sharing her own journey with scoliosis and
delivered three hundred copies to schools across Missouri. She has
also raised $30,000 to help scoliosis patients with expenses related to
treatment, organized a fashion show for teens with scoliosis, and suc-
ceeded in having September 1 designated as Scoliosis Awareness Day
by Missouri's governor. She is described by her principal as "active in our
school and community.... She is kind, caring, and considerate of others."
In addition to being an accomplished dancer and softball player, she is
a leader throughout the school. She was named Missouri's Top Youth
Volunteer in 2019 in the Prudential Spirit of Community Awards and
was crowned Miss Missouri's Outstanding Teen. You can learn more
about Catching the Curve at catchingthecurve.com/about.

NOMINATED BY DAVID GEURIN

**Graylen Kirby, 11; Liv Kirffe, 8; Mika Kirffe, 8; and McKensey Kirffe,
13—North Carolina:** While most five-year-olds request dolls and toys
for their birthdays, Graylen asked all of her family and friends for gift
cards for grocery stores when she was about to turn six. Why? She
used them to purchase ingredients to prepare a spaghetti dinner for

an overflow homeless shelter in her hometown so that she could help her most vulnerable neighbors in one of the coldest months of the year. Now, five years later, she continues her work each January by collecting supplies, cooking and serving dinner, and donating money. She has also enlisted the help of her three sisters, who assist with the planning, fundraising, shopping, and serving. Most recently, for her eleventh birthday, she decided she was old enough to work for the funds needed. So rather than asking for donations, she organized two fundraising events: one where she and her sisters took over as servers at a Tex-Mex restaurant one evening and worked for tips, and another where they hosted a shag-dancing demonstration fundraiser at a local club. Graylen and her sisters' efforts are now raising over $1,000 each year not just for dinner, but for purchasing the shelter supplies of pillows, blankets, snacks, water, medications, toiletries, and more. Not only that, but she wraps each of the items and delivers them to the shelter on her birthday so others can open up gifts.

NOMINATED BY SALEM KIRBY

Ethan Cordeiro, 15—Minnesota: Ethan has been involved in student-leadership roles since his elementary school days. He presented to the Wayzata School Board on the implementation of new technologies used to enhance learning and fielded questions on the topic from board members. He also appeared in recruitment videos for new staff at Greenwood Elementary School. Ethan was invited to speak at the 2018 Minnesota Elementary School Principal's Association Institute, where he was featured as the first student speaker and delivered a message highlighting small yet meaningful ways educators can engage with their students to encourage an ongoing passion for learning. He has done additional speaking on this topic for Wayzata Public Schools staff trainings as part of their Summer Tech Institute. He also delivered a graduation speech for the class of 2023 at Wayzata West Middle School. As he begins his high school career, Ethan continues to seek out additional student leadership opportunities both inside and outside of the classroom, while empowering his peers to do the same.

NOMINATED BY BRAD GUSTAFSON

Cameron Carlin, 20—Texas: Described as "intelligent, motivated, selfless, successful, and makes the lives of those around him, in a word, better." Cameron is a well-rounded young leader, excelling in sports, music, and community service. A few of his accolades include serving as a drum major, co-captain of the baseball team, a Boy Scout, tour guide, youth mentor, and volunteer at San Antonio's children's shelter. He has also been recognized by the Houston Astros and Trinity University for his service.

NOMINATED BY HAL BOWMAN

Multiage Learning Community at College Park Elementary, 6–9, South Carolina: After reading and researching about kids in need, this group of students decided that they wanted to take action. The students created ideas for how to help, formulated a pitch and presentation to present to the school's administration, and then set out to work. What was formed was Kids Inspired & Determined to Serve (K.I.D.S.). They created and sold handmade greeting cards and calendars to sell then used the money raised to help others. Their first round raised $1,360. Half of the money was donated to Water Mission, which helps people in developing countries and disaster areas get clean water. The other half was used to purchase new books for sick children in hospitals. They continue to fundraise and support kids in need. If you would like to learn more and find ways you can help, visit bit.ly/2RO0E5M.

NOMINATED BY JUDY RAINEY

Gianni D'Ascensio, 10—New Jersey: After noticing that students were inappropriately writing on school property, Gianni wanted to find a solution to the problem. He approached his school counselor and principal to share his idea to get positive messages to the students in his school and encourage students to write for positive reasons. He envisioned a place in the building where students could visit to grab a handwritten positive message and also add one of their own as well. They found a "take one, leave one" template and the rest was history! Gianni created a video, with the help of the school counselor, explaining to his peers why he thought the school needed this and what the display would offer students. The video was shared with the entire school. Gianni's leadership inspired peers, teachers, and administrators to write messages and add positivity to someone's day. In fact, it led to a similar display being created for the adults of the school!

NOMINATED BY KRISTEN KRIES

Alyssa Swaby, 14—Florida: Alyssa has always had a heart for helping others, and she has shown it consistently in her young life. In addition to spending much of her free time volunteering at the ASPCA, she built a website to help the dogs there get adopted. She also demonstrated her digital skills at school as a leader in the Code Club, where she was asked to be a part of a video introducing a local business, Codecraft Labs, to other students who may want to learn to code. Her hard work and efforts afforded her a spot in the National Honor Society, where she served as president, organizing events and fundraisers for the group.

NOMINATED BY DEB JAMES

Maitreyi Shrikhande, 16—Iowa: Maitreyi loves to give back to her community. Starting when she was in the third grade, she would go back to her old primary campus and read to four-year-olds. From there, she has continued to find ways to volunteer at places like the Figge Art Museum and the Quad City Youth Ensemble. Now in high school, she has grown her leadership skills in a number of ways. Most notably, she volunteers at the local hospital each week, where she plays the cello in the lobby, works the front desk, and delivers art made by elementary students to patients. She has also given a TEDxYouth talk on volunteering (youtu.be/LVaLaKSvF8w) called "The Unexpected Outcomes of Volunteering" and serves on several organizing committees for community events such as Teens for Tomorrow and One Human Family.

NOMINATED BY EVAN MOSIER

Colton Ehle, 15; Hunter Ehle, 18; and Lexi Ehle, 18—Indiana: In the fall of 2014, after being inspired by Kid President's call on social media for kids to do something to change the world, twins Hunter and Lexi (then thirteen years old) and their brother Colton (nine) decided to try and do something to help the homeless in their community. They reached out to the Fort Wayne Rescue Mission to ask about their greatest needs. What they found was that as winter approached there was a huge need for socks to keep the feet of the homeless warm, clean, and healthy. The siblings decided to start a sock drive at their school during the month of October, which they called SOCKTOBER. They made posters, fliers, videos, and social media posts to promote it. Their initial goal for the first year was to collect 250 pairs. They ended up collecting 2,280 pairs of socks! They continued the sock drive the following year and collected 3,090 pairs of socks. In 2016, when Hunter and Lexi moved on to high school, Colton excitedly took the helm and brought SOCKTOBER to a whole new level with new promotions and challenges. The efforts collected 4,833 pairs of socks. Over the next few years, Colton continued to improve and grow the project to help the homeless and collected so many socks, that his drive alone put socks on the feet of every homeless person in three large counties in Indiana. In 2018, his drive had grown so large that Colton decided to add other items to it. In the end, he collected over 14,000 HUGS (hats, underwear, gloves, and socks) for the homeless in his community, proving kids truly can make a difference!

NOMINATED BY HOLLY EHLE

WHEN KIDS LEAD

WHEN KIDS LEAD

AN ADULT`S GUIDE TO
INSPIRING, EMPOWERING, AND GROWING
YOUNG LEADERS

Todd Nesloney and Adam Dovico

When Kids Lead: An Adult's Guide to Inspiring, Empowering, and Growing Young Leaders
© 2020 Todd Nesloney and Adam Dovico

This book is available at special discounts when purchased in quantity for educational purposes or as premiums, promotions, or fundraisers. For inquiries and details, contact the publisher at books@daveburgessconsulting.com.

Published by Dave Burgess Consulting, Inc.
San Diego, CA
DaveBurgessConsulting.com

Library of Congress Control Number: 2020935891
Paperback ISBN: 978-1-951600-24-2
Ebook ISBN: 978-1-951600-25-9

Cover and interior design by Liz Schreiter

ADAM

For my sons, Ryder and Maddox, who
hold the future in their hands.

TODD

For those who have never felt like a leader. Regardless
of what you've been told in the past, you are a leader.
Prove them wrong. Lead bravely.

For Lissette, for helping remind me who I am.

CONTENTS

FOREWORD

JOSHUA WILLIAMS

I n 2005, I started Joshua's Heart Foundation, a 501(c)(3) aimed at creating young changemakers who would stomp out world hunger and poverty. Still only four and a half years old at the time, my eyes were set on being an upstander, and not a bystander, in my community. Fueled by passion and supported by the adults in my life, I set forth to make an impact and show that kids can be leaders. Eternal gratitude goes out to my family and teachers, who molded my journey by modeling entrepreneurship and helping me find my own voice at home and in the classroom. This large group of women in my life led through character and work ethic. As they influenced my development over the years, their impact remains an integral part of me. Now a college student, I am sitting in a transitional period between childhood and adulthood, and I can clearly see that the leadership skills gained from these adult influencers in my life become even more relevant as I move forward into the next chapter of my life.

Since the inception of Joshua's Heart, we have delivered over two million pounds of food and raised over $1.2 million for the homeless all through the power of youth leadership. What started out as me asking a few friends to help give back has grown to over 50,000 youth volunteers seeking radical change for the world. Joshua's Heart has continued to grow to now include weekly food distribution, a food pantry, cooking classes, a backpack program, food drives, fundraisers, and more. Each of these events or programs are run by youth teams who coordinate and execute a plan that they develop themselves. And I'm proud that my fellow young colleagues and I have shown the power of youth leadership and the impact it can have on a community and beyond over the past fourteen years.

Our success was no happenstance, though. Kids see the world differently than adults. Albeit naïve and usually filled with innocence, a child has a creativity and imagination that often doesn't know any limits. And with a combination of self-awareness, adult guidance, and unbounded creativity, kids do become leaders. In today's society, young leadership continues to advance. We witness it in youth taking the reins in business, social issues, and media.

When Kids Lead illustrates the importance and value of cultivating youth leadership in our schools, homes, teams, and clubs. Todd and Adam outline the critical role adults play in nurturing this development through personal narratives, practical experiences, and relatable examples. In an era when youth are frequently criticized and stereotyped for being connected to phones and disconnected from society, we cannot forget the potential that lies inside each child that can be brought out by a devoted adult.

To move humanity forward and make global shifts we must allow for the creation of a new wave of leaders who are young, creative, and hungry for change. And whether it is Joshua's Heart Foundation or any other young world-changer's movement, business, charity—or just a kid sitting in your classroom looking to share a thought—I urge adults to be mindful of the future and how you can set it up to be bright. Todd and Adam recognize this societal necessity with their call for acceptance of the power that kids can have when adults allow them to dream, develop, and lead.

INTRODUCTION

A leader is a person that stands up for other people and a person who is responsible, trustworthy, kind, a helper, and smart. A leader sometimes has to say yes, but also at times they have to say no. Leaders think before they act, and they motivate other people around them.

—BENNETT, AGE 10

Recognizing that leadership plays a role in what most people define as success, we all look for ways to become strong effective leaders through many means—workshops, programs, and motivational speeches, to name a few. Just think of the countless leadership books at your disposal. But how many of those books are targeted to developing leadership in our youth?

Very few. That's why we wrote this book. We want to show that our children possess the same leadership virtues that society lauds in adults. Honesty, courage, empathy, kindness, fairness, creativity, enthusiasm, selflessness, and integrity are just a handful of characteristics often associated with the adult leaders we admire. Look around and you will see there are children everywhere who possess these same desirable characteristics.

Classical leadership will point to successful inventors, artists, and entrepreneurs as those we should follow. While those types of figures do contribute to the overall narrative, leadership is not about being famous, making money, or winning awards but rather making a difference in the lives of others. Throughout this book, we acknowledge young leadership as defined by demonstration of the characteristics listed above and share ideas for how to help grow those characteristics in all of our kids.

We also highlight the importance of children having an emboldened adult who realizes and cultivates their leadership potential. This book is specifically geared toward adults who work with children. Educators, parents, coaches, and mentors—we want you to realize that children rely on you to guide them along the way. They expect adults to provide encouragement, feedback, resources, and celebration. Accepting that duty is not always easy or desired but, if we are to lay the groundwork for our society's future through our youth, adult support is vital.

We both believe in this work because we have lived the principles in this book firsthand as teachers and principals. Adam was a teacher for over a decade at schools at the elementary, middle school, and college levels, including the renowned Ron Clark Academy. He then served as a principal at a Title 1 school in North Carolina and has since taught model lessons in kindergarten through twelfth-grade classrooms all over the country. He has been recognized as an award recipient of the Japan Fulbright Memorial Fund Teacher Program and the Southern Poverty Law Center Teaching Tolerance program. Todd was a teacher for seven years and served as a principal at a Title 1 school in Texas for an additional five. He currently serves as the director of culture and strategic leadership for the Texas Elementary

Principals and Supervisors Association. In addition to presenting two TEDx talks, Todd has been recognized by John C. Maxwell as a top-ten finalist for the 2018 Transformational Leadership Award, by President Barack Obama as a Champion of Change, and by the National School Board Association as a 20 to Watch honoree.

Our many and differed experiences have allowed us to gain an appreciation for the immense abilities children possess. Together, we will introduce you to a myriad of the programs, lessons, experiences, and anecdotes that have formulated our belief that children can lead. To tell this narrative, we will use a collective voice through much of the book but also share stories unique to each of us. Such instances of first-person storytelling will be signaled by a labeling of our individual names to indicate the speaker.

So what happens when kids lead?

Many perhaps think of leadership as requiring transformative change and therefore can call to mind only a few examples of kids leading. One such leader might be Louis Braille, who at fifteen and while attending France's Royal Institute for Blind Youth, developed a coding system that allowed blind people to read and write quickly. His system, now known simply as braille, has remained essentially unchanged since its creation.

But leadership manifests itself on many levels, and a broader conception of what it entails illustrates only more the importance of cultivating all these virtues in children. Consider Cassidy Goldstein. At age eleven, Goldstein solved a problem to a common issue that people around the world face: what to do with a broken crayon. When she grew frustrated that broken or worn-down crayons are difficult to color with, she took an old floral water tube and created the Crayon Holder, which extends the life of crayons, protects hands from getting dirty, and helps children who have a difficult time gripping crayons.

Or consider Mari Copeny, whom you may know better as "Little Miss Flint." In 2016, she wrote a letter to President Obama urging him to meet with her and her community while attending a rally in Washington, D.C., to discuss the Flint water crisis. Copeny's young voice was acknowledged, and President Obama ended up visiting Flint and signing off on $100 million to help repair the city's water system. She continues to be an advocate for her community and is a youth ambassador for the Women's March, the People's Climate March, and Equality for HER.

These young inventors, entrepreneurs, and activists have both inspired and changed the world around them. But there are many more children just like them sitting in your classroom, living in your home, or participating in your team or club. They are waiting for that moment to share their ideas, help others, make an impression on someone, or take the stage.

To provide children with a platform for action, we must first listen. Don't dismiss children when they have a dream or idea. Walt Disney said, "Our greatest natural resource is the minds of our children." Adults have a responsibility to teach the skills and provide the resources necessary to develop the potential leadership in every child. And when a child is ready to independently exhibit that leadership, it is fitting that the adults involved step aside for the child to take control.

We further challenge you to look closely at our most marginalized youth—children of color, children living in poverty, children with disabilities, and children identifying as LGBTQ+—to find ways to ensure that they are receiving practice with leadership actions and skills that in more privileged communities are provided as a matter of course. To move forward as a society, we must hear from all leaders, especially those who historically have not been given a voice. When we begin providing all students these opportunities, everyone (including adults) is better for it. Cultivating leadership in children results in a world of benefits:

- We uphold the ideals of a society in which a balance between individual rights and commitment and responsibility toward others can be maintained.
- We achieve the principles of fairness and equity for all people.
- We develop in children virtues such as curiosity, responsibility, perseverance, and the willingness to experiment and fail.
- We build a bridge between society and school, where the desired outcomes of a productive citizen are met through the teachings and opportunities that school presents.
- We make available an avenue for recognition and success for students who are marginalized by traditional academic measures or socioeconomic factors.

These critical, coveted objectives guided the writing of this book. We will share practical, tried-and-true ideas for promoting leadership development—implementing SPECIAL, planning student-led conferences, making available diverse literature, encouraging passion projects, and more—that will show you how to inspire, empower, and grow young leaders in our classrooms, homes, teams, and communities. You'll see that there's not one single right way to develop leaders. Leadership comes in all shapes and sizes, as we know from experiencing the adults around us each day. There are boisterous leaders, quiet leaders, leaders who wait until the right moment to step in, and leaders who charge at the forefront of change.

We believe that each of us is a leader. Unfortunately, many kids are left with dormant potential because they lack exposure to adults who believe it's possible for kids to lead—or for particular kids to lead. Let's make a commitment today that we will look deep within each of our students, our children, and light the flame that is waiting to be lit. Let's give them a chance to shine bright for others to see.

PART
1

HOW LEADERSHIP TRAINING WORKS

Leaders are people whose actions have a positive influence on others. They are people with growth mindsets, not only for themselves, but also for the groups that they lead.

—COLTON, AGE 14

We wrote this book with two functions in mind: to build awareness of the numerous possibilities that exist for students to exercise leadership within schools and to explain how to train students to capitalize on these opportunities. Before we delve into the when and where of promoting leadership possibilities in our schools, teams, clubs, and organizations, we will first look at how this promotion can be done and why it is important.

We start with the mechanics of leadership because we have found that many adults are not comfortable with the explicit teaching of leadership skills. Frankly, we teach what we feel equipped to teach. Take a football coach, for instance. On many youth teams, coaches teach the mechanics of playing football: blocking, tackling, running, and catching. While these are important skills to learn, excelling at them will create effective individual players, not successful teams. How often do we see coaches teaching explicit leadership skills, like integrity, fairness, and selflessness, that can yield teamwork? What would it look like if all coaches valued teaching leadership as much as teaching ball skills?

In most educator preparation programs, there are no courses that teach how to instill student leadership into everyday teaching. If anything, leadership discussions are typically about how you as the teacher can be a leader in the classroom. As a result, teachers enter the profession being comfortable dispersing content knowledge and engaging students, but they miss out on the opportunity to create student-centered classrooms where kids are leading discussions, taking ownership over their own learning, and building social and career skills.

In our first chapter, we lay out practical, proven ideas for how to inspire, empower, and grow young leaders by detailing how you can equip students with the tools and skill sets needed for effective leadership.

1

BUILDING SKILLS

As a leader, you don't have to be someone rich, famous, or iconic. A leader is someone who isn't perfect, but instead they are someone who isn't afraid to try and grow as a person. A leader is someone who isn't afraid to let themselves be vulnerable by sharing their experiences and mistakes in the hopes that someone else listening may learn and grow from them. A leader can be someone from anywhere, just grasping the chance to try and change the world by being that one person who makes a wonderful impact on someone's life. A leader is a spark of hope.

—ELISE, AGE 14

At twelve years old, Freeman Hrabowski found himself arrested by police on the streets of Birmingham, Alabama, one of a group of children peacefully marching for equal rights during the Civil Rights Movement. In what became known as the Children's Crusade, young protesters endured police brutality, violence, and jail as they took on leadership roles in one of the most divisive eras in our country's history.

Hrabowski, now recognized as one of the most influential leaders in the world as the president of the University of Maryland, Baltimore County, attributes to the adults in his life his success as a mathematician, educator, and advocate. As a child, he was surrounded by adults who taught him vital skills that aided him not only in his younger years but also throughout his adulthood.

He credits Reverend John T. Porter and other leaders of the Sixth Street Avenue Baptist Church for modeling and teaching him speaking and thinking skills. During youth fellowship meetings, young boys and girls would discuss readings that developed critical thinking skills with topics questioning how things could be different and exploring what American democracy means. By allowing Hrabowski and other children to discuss such issues, these youth were shaping their own minds on how to become active members of society and bring about change.

Freeman Hrabowski also tells of the reaction of his high school principal, who was forced to put the students out of school after their participation in the Children's Crusade. The principal had several of the suspended students read Henry David Thoreau's short essay, *Civil Disobedience*. Instead of looking down on the young activists and making the episode into something shameful, the principal called the entire school together and conducted a session in the "same manner that he did for the induction of the Honor Society." Hrabowski recalls that the principal was "determined that those of us being suspended would know it was a badge of courage."[1]

The skills that Hrabowski learned as a child were taught intentionally and wisely by the adults around him. In analyzing his story,

---

1 Hrabowski, F.A., Mosnier, J. & Civil Rights History Project, U.S. (2011) *Freeman A. Hrabowski oral history interview conducted by Joseph Mosnier in Baltimore, Maryland. [Pdf] Retrieved from the Library of Congress, loc.gov/item/2015669131/.*

it is clear that the adults recognized that allowing the children to read, discuss, and think critically about matters of importance is crucial for building a stronger future society. Further, the actions of Hrabowski's principal were exemplary. He selected a text for the suspended students to read that aligned to their mission and focus and also held up the group of activists for others to see as a model from which to learn.

As adults, we can find countless moments each day to be intentional in building leadership skills in our students. Hrabowski learned courage, selflessness, and integrity from the lessons his adult mentors presented to him. This book aims to present ways and means by which every adult can do the same for our youth. We would like to start by presenting a system that serves as a foundation on which to build many other skills. You can look at it as the groundwork for what could later become leadership traits such as kindness, empathy, and confidence. Many would call these soft, interpersonal, or real-world skills. No matter what you label them, these traits are a good place to start.

All societies across the world and throughout history have created norms and expectations for interactions. Greetings, body language, and word usage are all dictated by culture and unwritten rules. And while commonalities can be found among cultures and societies at times, wide variances also exist. Learning and implementing your own society's customs while simultaneously educating yourself on others' is complex work. That's why it is important to start while young.

To help guide this work, Adam created a system called SPECIAL. This acronym is based on the social interactions widely taught in Western business acumen: shaking hands, posture, eye contact, charm, introducing yourself, asking a question, and leaning in and listening. Detailed instruction for teaching each of the seven elements follows.

To teach children how to shake hands, begin by modeling holding the right hand out and forming a letter *L*. Indicate the web of the hand and model that when the two webs meet, the hands clasp. Explain that we aim to touch the webs first to avoid a fingertip shake. From there, work with students on the strength and duration of the handshake.

In addition to demonstrating the traditional sense of good posture—standing up straight and holding the shoulders back and the chest out—model effective speaking and listening posture. Hands should be either out in front of the body, on the side of the body, or behind the back. Tell students to avoid putting their hands into pockets or crossing their arms, and show how swaying can be distracting to the listener.

Encourage students to maintain eye contact with the person they are meeting throughout the duration of the encounter, even if the other person does not do it in return. It gives the impression of confidence and assures the other person that the student is fully attentive.

Effective execution of charming behaviors adds to memorability and standing out. Subtle gestures like a smile, raised eyebrow, head nod, or chuckle are all behaviors that carry with them elements of charm. Model how these small expressions can be done in a way that shows you are listening and engaged, without being distracting.

Stress to students the importance of introducing themselves properly. Articulating a greeting and name ("Hi. I'm Adam.") breaks the ice upon meeting someone new. The practice customarily leads to the other person returning the gesture.

Encourage students to take the introduction a step further by transitioning into asking a question of the new person. Help students compile a toolbox of questions, such as "How was your day?" or "How are you?" or "Can you tell me about yourself?" This will assist them in the otherwise difficult task of initiating conversation.

As someone is speaking, a slight leaning in provides the body language needed to show engagement in the conversation. Model how active listening facilitates a follow-up question. For example, if someone states that he or she enjoys playing basketball, it would be good to ask a question about that person's involvement in the sport.

While the individual elements of SPECIAL may be taught in isolation, the application is invariably mingled. We encourage you to demonstrate the overlap and connectedness of these skills as they are being taught. For example, when shaking someone's hand, it is customary to look the other person in the eye while maintaining a confident posture and introducing yourself.

Further, it is imperative that as you teach these skills, you integrate discussions on individualism, culture, and ability. In some cultures, it would be deemed disrespectful for a child to look an adult in the eye. In other cultures, bowing would take the place of shaking hands. You might meet someone who prefers not to have physical contact or is not able to stand or speak. These conversations must lead into practice so that students understand that there is no one approach for interacting with other people.

The adults in Freeman Hrabowski's life provided explicit lessons teaching him the skills that helped develop him into a leader. If the SPECIAL system and what it represents are important to you, be deliberate in the teaching of the skills addressed. Here are a few suggestions to guide how you deliver these lessons:

- Model: Show students what proper skills look like. In addition to your demonstration, bring in guests or show videos that can lead to discussion or analysis.
- Find opportunities: It is vital that students have the chance to practice the skills. Carve out or find natural times to implement practice.
- Immediate feedback: If a student incorrectly executes a skill when implementing, indicate the error and have them immediately try it again.

- Set high expectations: Just because the learners are children does not mean they are any less capable. Set a high bar so they have somewhere to reach for.
- Challenge: As students become more comfortable with the basics, continue to question and challenge their understanding by presenting different scenarios.
- Connect leadership lessons: Discuss how building interpersonal skills connects to leadership traits such as courage, kindness, enthusiasm, and empathy.

As with SPECIAL, many of the leadership strategies we provide throughout the book can be executed using these same delivery tips. What we hope you will find is that no matter the leadership lesson or skill you are aiming to teach, you will discover that as adults, we wield tremendous power when it comes to inspiring, empowering, and growing young leaders.

CONCLUSION

TODD

I love finding those students who have yet to believe that they are leaders, students who have allowed their own doubt and insecurities keep them from reaching their full potential.

I remember when I first met Ray in 4th grade. He was an incredibly timid, yet mischievous, student. He had moved schools many times and had difficulty building relationships not only with his peers but also with adults.

Immediately I could sense the potential that lay within Ray. As we built a stronger relationship, I began to identify his quirks and strengths and spent time daily pouring encouragement into him.

I can so vividly recall a conversation I had with Ray early on after he had made some poor decisions on the playground. I said, "Ray,

I know you have incredible qualities in you that would make you a fantastic leader, but you continually try to hide them away and instead of drawing people into you, it seems like you're more interested in pushing them away." And it's what he said next that broke my heart. He said, "Mr. Nesloney, we both know that I will never be a leader. I'm not the smartest, I'm not the most athletic, and my last teacher told me that the only thing she could see in my future was a prison cell. I think she's right. There's nothing that makes me good."

Sometimes as an educator you are faced with those moments where you have to draw on every ounce of strength not to cry when a child breaks your heart. I put my hands on his shoulders and looked straight into his eyes and said, "Ray, I want you to remember what I'm about to tell you. No one is in control of your future except for you. And the young man I have gotten to know over the last few weeks is witty, creative, and a natural leader. The only thing you're missing is the ability to see yourself the way I see you. I'm going to remind you every day of just how incredible you are until you believe it too."

Over the next year and a half, I spent time every week not only reminding Ray of the qualities I saw in him, but also providing him opportunities to lead, whether that was joining class discussion, being group leader, running something to the office, or helping out in a younger grade level classroom. It wasn't until about eight years later that Ray returned to my doorway and let me know that that one conversation where I told him I would remind him daily gave him hope enough to learn to believe in himself as well. Sometimes the leadership skills, or reminders of potential, that we speak into a child's life don't manifest immediately. But it doesn't mean we give up.

ADAM

During my freshman year of high school, I was for all intents and purposes a decent student. I consistently made As and Bs, played sports, joined clubs, and was class president. For a big school, teachers knew who I was and most adults considered me a leader among my peers.

In World History class freshman year, we sat in five straight rows, about eight students deep. I was toward the back of one of the rows, which I later found out was teacher code for "he's not going to cause trouble, so he can sit in the back." One day we were taking a test on the Aztecs and Mayans, and I had finished the test fairly quickly. I was checking over my answers when my friend Samantha, who sat behind me, whispered, "What did you get for number eight?"

I ignored her at first, but she asked again. I looked up and saw Mr. Chirak walking toward the door to check something, so I quickly turned around and told her what I wrote. She confirmed she had written the same thing. Before I knew it, we had checked a few more answers. I figured all was good though because the teacher sat down and went on with his business.

At the end of class, we were to turn in our tests on the way out. When Samantha and I went to turn ours in, Mr. Chirak took our tests, looked at us with disappointment and anger in his face, and said, "I didn't think I would have to worry about this from you two."

We both put our heads down, knowing we had gotten busted. I tried mumbling something about how we were just checking on something for later in the day, but he wasn't dumb. He put our tests in a separate pile and we walked out.

I was so ashamed and embarrassed, though appreciative he didn't call us out in front of the entire class. I had worked so hard to establish leadership within my freshman class and the school, and a stupid mistake like cheating was going to ruin it all.

The next morning, I went to his room before the school day started. I didn't have much of a game plan in mind, but I knew I needed to apologize. I walked in, and it was almost as if he was expecting me. He told me to sit down. He explained that he didn't know why I did it, but he knew I was better than that. After I apologized, he told me that I would get an F for this test, but he did acknowledge that I had owned up to the mistake and that my admission mattered to him.

I appreciated his mercy in the situation, but I was even more thankful for what he did after that day. Mr. Chirak never held the situation against me and never brought it up again. I think back and realize that he even went out of his way to help me build my confidence back up in class by choosing me to be a leader with several activities and projects we did as the year went on.

When I became a teacher, I never forgot how Mr. Chirak dealt with that situation. He was firm in his actions when I deserved it but also nurturing when it came to showing me how to bounce back from a setback. I've had a number of students over the years who I caught cheating, and I always tried to approach the situation similarly. I help them to understand that they did not do the right thing in this situation, but I also try to create a leadership lesson out of this. I want them to learn that leaders know how to have difficult conversations, when to apologize, when to own their consequences, and how to get better from them.

LEADERS' REFLECTION QUESTIONS:

1. What leadership skills do you value most? How can you develop them within your students on a daily basis?

2. Reflect on a time where you had an unexpected opportunity to teach a student a leadership lesson. What did you do? How did that student react?

> Share on social media how your students are building leadership skills. Use the hashtag #WhenKidsLead.

2

CULTIVATING CHARACTER

A leader is someone who teaches others the right thing, even if they don't get it. A leader is a person who perseveres and who helps others be leaders. Leaders set the example. They make mistakes and teach others how to avoid them. They're someone who shows respect and deserves it. They help you become who you want to be, no matter how good you are at something. They don't take "no" or "I can't." They take "I can" and "I will."

—FINN, AGE 10

eing a leader, whether desired or not, can be exhausting. Eyes and ears are constantly on you, examining your words and actions. The smallest missteps can be questioned, and self-doubt can set in. At times, those who wish to be in your shoes may try to bring you down.

But leadership can also be empowering and bring about change. A leader has the ability to alter trajectories, shift mindsets, and revolutionize outcomes. When their fuel tank is nearing empty, leaders know how to use every last drop of gas to fuel those around them. It is ultimately their character that refuels their tank and shifts them to the next gear. Their ability to persevere through difficult times inspires others. It's their understanding of their surroundings and the transparency in their actions that makes them relatable to others. Even when weakened, a leader has the ability to show others how to overcome adversity and do the right thing.

At Adam's college graduation, he had the pleasure and honor of hearing then Secretary of State Colin Powell deliver the commencement address. During the speech, Powell said:

> In my profession, character is perhaps the most important trait we seek and expect in our leaders. Character which inspires trust in others, character which gives confidence to others to follow you into the darkest night. Character which keeps you pointed toward true north no matter what winds or waves come to try to push you off course onto the shoals of doubt, dishonesty and despair. Character which always presses you to do the right thing. . . . Do the right thing, even when you get no credit for it, even if you get hurt by doing the right thing. Do the right thing when no one is watching or will ever know about it. You will always know. (May 17, 2004)

So if Powell is right that a leader's character calls the leader to "do the right thing," it begs the question: Are leaders born or do they learn to do the right thing?

We believe that a young leader's ability to do the right thing comes from a moral compass that is ever developing through experiences, lessons, and knowledge. As a parent, teacher, coach, or mentor, we have the opportunity and responsibility to promote character development in our young leaders.

We firmly come down not only on the side that leaders can and do learn how to do the right thing but that character itself can be taught and cultivated. It's not enough to train kids to act like leaders; they have to *become* leaders. You can train them to cut through problems, but a saw needs to be continually sharpened to be effective and resilient. Therefore, teaching leadership must include fostering character development.

Let's start with some practical ways to begin building character before delving into a scenario in more detail.

REINFORCE THE POSITIVE

When you see a child demonstrating virtuous character traits, let that individual know that you recognize the effort. This action affirms the behavior and makes the child more likely to replicate it in the future. Be sure to give children the language of good character as well: the more they are exposed to something, the greater the chance they will remember and embrace it. When our schools and homes display visual representations of good character, for example, we are sending a message to our children (and a reminder to ourselves) that these words matter. Positive quotes on posters and murals are an easy and effective way to display such words.

When Adam was a principal, he teamed up with his art teacher to refurbish old mirrors acquired from a Habitat for Humanity ReStore. On the mirrors, the teacher pasted cut outs of graduation caps and gowns along with positive quotes such as "If you dream it, you can do it!" and "Be the best you that you can be!" The mirrors were hung in the main hallway so that as students walked down the hall they couldn't help but pause and look into one to see themselves in a cap and gown and be reminded to work hard and be the best they can be. Todd's school placed mirrors in the hallways as well, but instead of graduation caps and gowns, they embellished them with phrases such as "I am fierce," "I am brave," and "I am enough." The kids would look in the mirrors and see their reflection along with words of affirmation.

HAVE DISCUSSIONS SURROUNDING CHARACTER

To develop character in students, many schools use a school counselor, implement a social-emotional learning program, or teach a curriculum that includes lessons around demonstrating positive character. But for character education to truly take hold, it has to be infused in the lives of the kids throughout their day. Teachers, don't miss out on opportunities to integrate character education into your everyday lessons when you discuss characters in a story or people in history. Encourage families at home to discuss what positive character looks like in the student's family and household. If faith is important to a family, suggest that they draw upon the writings of their religion to base discussions and principles. Coaches of athletes can look to revered coaches like John Wooden and Pat Summit, who have provided many of the most inspirational phrases, quotes, and speeches about character and leadership out there. Don't reduce cultivating character to an item to check off of a curriculum to-do list; work to infuse it throughout the culture of your school and your students' lives.

We offer this word of advice: too often we point to figures like Martin Luther King, Jr., Gandhi, or Mother Teresa when we discuss what a high moral compass and powerful leadership look like. While they are certainly excellent models to follow, they can come off as unrelatable for a child. Seek out examples of young leaders and "ordinary" people to study in both history and current events so students can better comprehend their own possibility for making an impact on the world. Remember that what's important is the action performed—focusing on the heroic stature of people can make their actions seem remote and inaccessible to kids.

FACILITATE SELF-REFLECTION

Mistakes and failures are a part of becoming a leader of positive character. For young leaders to recognize this truth, it is important to offer them opportunities to reflect upon experiences and guide them with questions that help them conclude that their stumble will actually lead to greater understanding in the future. While it is tempting and perhaps even convenient to "save" a student from a learning experience, we must allow safe failures to occur or else children will develop a false sense of immunity.

At the same time, it's important to present young leaders with real-life situations that may require their character to be tested. When we role-play moral dilemmas, we are more apt to make the right decision when a situation actually arises. For example, leading up to a big test, a student offers a classmate a copy of it with the answers coded. What should the classmate do? Have students practice what they would say and do in tough situations, and use those experiences to facilitate greater self-reflection about why character matters. Also, identify accountability partners that students can turn to for feedback when needed. By promoting self-reflection early on, we are showing children that it is okay to speak up and call on their friends when needed. Ultimately, we are equipping children with both intrapersonal (self-reflection) and interpersonal (discussion) discernment for successfully overcoming moral dilemmas.

As adults, we know that not every leader becomes influential or powerful through righteous means. Some leaders compromised their moral compass along the way and, despite dishonorable actions, were able to use deception to place themselves in positions of power. To avoid a future that repeats the past, we must take responsibility for the children in front of us now. The impressionable youth in our classrooms today are more determined than ever to make the world a better place, and their flowing ideas are vast and sincere. It is our duty to help them achieve their honorable ends through character-building means.

When a child wants to lead a project that boosts recycling or a club that allows LGBTQ+ students to feel safer, ask them how you can help. If a student comes up to you wondering what they can do to help a classmate with cancer, start a conversation. And if your son or daughter comes home explaining that someone at school is bullying another student, talk to them about what they can do about it.

Adults hold so much influence and leverage in a child's ability to lead. They need to be there to listen, guide, mold, and pick a young leader up when down.

BOOKS AND LEADERSHIP

Books can change a life. They open up worlds for us to explore and learn more about not only ourselves but others as well. Books allow us the opportunity to feel less alone and to connect more deeply. Books also build empathy. We always question when someone tells us they're not a reader or don't like reading. The truth is there's no such thing. There are only kids who haven't yet found that book that breaks their heart. That book that they can't put down. That book that as soon as they've finished they must talk to someone else about it because it moved them so much.

We can begin to find such books by relinquishing the antiquated idea that children (and adults, for that matter) are truly reading only if they're holding an on-level chapter book in their hands. Whether it's a picture book, graphic novel, comic strip, magazine, audiobook, or any other material, reading is reading.

We want to particularly note the significance of using picture books with kids (and adults) of all ages. We think of picture books being appropriate solely for a younger elementary classroom. But we forget the amount of instruction that can take place through the imagery, foreshadowing, text structure, cross-curricular content, and lessons of a picture book. In reality, there are far more uses for a picture book in a secondary classroom or adult education environment than a younger elementary classroom!

We also believe that kids can't see themselves as readers if the adults around them aren't modelling reading. We know how busy life is, but always remember that we all have time for exactly what we make time for. If reading and creating that love of reading is important to us, we'll make time for it. As a school principal, Todd made reading a priority on campus through daily book talks during announcements, setting aside budget money to ensure growth of classroom and school library collections yearly, executing events like Book Prom and Secret Society of Readers, sharing in his email signature what he was reading, gifting books for holidays and birthdays, always carrying a book, reading to classes monthly, and many more ways. Reading can't be an activity we encourage only during reading instruction in class.

TODD

I hated reading as a child. It's not that it wasn't easy for me, it's just that there was never anything that interested me.

When I was in fifth grade, my mother took me to our school's Scholastic Book Fair. I was dreading it and begged her not to waste her time. But my mother, being the great mother she was, didn't give me a choice.

As I perused the shelves at the book fair, as always, nothing seemed to stand out to me, until while scanning books, I stopped in my tracks. Immediately I was drawn to the cover of a book featuring an illustration of a boy changing into a lizard. I had never imagined myself being drawn into a story of teenagers who could morph and a secret alien invasion. But then again, being the hardcore Power Rangers fan I was, how could I not see this coming?

Over the next few years I consumed every single book in the Animorphs book series by K. A. Applegate (now known as Katherine Applegate, of the *The One and Only Ivan* fame). I would save my money and count down the days until the next book in the series was released and beg my grandmother to take me to the store to buy them. I was hooked.

Role models serve as an important piece in connecting students with books and developing a love of reading. One of Adam's close friends and former colleagues, Dr. Alan Brown, has a deep interest in the culture of sports in schools and in connecting contemporary literacies to students' extracurricular interests. He created an after-school middle school group called The Sports Literacy Program, in which he and former Wake Forest University football captain Wendell Dunn met weekly with their group to read contemporary adolescent sports literature. Alan picked high-interest books and even hosted a visit from author Robert Lipsyte when the group read *The Contender*.

The students in this group were eighth-grade African American boys. For them, it was more than a book about boxing that hooked them; it was seeing that a Division 1 football player who looked like them was holding and reading the same book. These boys worshipped Wendell. And though building a love of reading was certainly his primary objective, he was simultaneously modeling leadership traits such as responsibility (showing up each week), respect (speaking to others kindly), and engagement (actively participating) for these young men. Wendell would also visit the boys in class during the week and check in with their teachers to see how they were doing. It's this type of adult mentoring and modeling that made the Sports Literacy Program so successful. If you want to learn more about the program, you can visit its website at sportsliteracy.org/paisley-sports-literacy-program.

Perhaps most importantly, we believe that part of developing character is introducing rich and diverse texts, letting students learn alongside characters from all walks of life. Some characters they can see themselves in; in other characters they see nothing about themselves. Choose titles by authors who come from diverse backgrounds (migrant, Muslim, African, etc.) and who can speak and write authentically about their characters' experiences.

The importance of introducing your students to diverse texts cannot be understated. It is the responsibility of each of us to ensure that the literature we are recommending to our students reflects the kind of world they'll be entering, with characters with rich stories and culturally appropriate backgrounds. Some of you may be reading this and thinking, "Well, I've got a pretty diverse lineup of books in my school/classroom." What we always have to remind ourselves is that if all of our books with African American characters depict them as enslaved persons or civil rights activists, our books are not diverse—they are perpetuating a stereotype. If all of our books with Muslim characters have them as the antagonist or fighting in a war, our books are not diverse—they are perpetuating a stereotype. Until our students can see these historically marginalized characters as the hero of the story, our books aren't truly diverse.

When our children are exposed to truly diverse literature, they are building capacity to better understand and function in an ever increasingly connected world. They are developing compassion and a voice to speak up against injustices, standing beside those fighting for equality, and building appreciation for those who may be different from them.

As a first grader, Adam's son Ryder had a deaf girl in his class. He had never interacted with a deaf person before, so Adam and his wife bought *Helen's Big World: The Life of Helen Keller* by Doreen Rappaport and Matt Tavares to use as an introduction. Through Keller's story, Ryder developed an empathetic understanding of what it means to be deaf. He ended up becoming deeply interested in deaf culture and checking out from his school's media center books on sign language and featuring deaf characters. These types of books became staples for him, and this passion for learning about deaf culture all started with one book.

CONCLUSION

We believe books can change a life. We've seen it firsthand, not only in our own lives but in the lives of students we've served. We hope you make time today to check out a book that makes you a little uncomfortable. Read a book that challenges your thinking or long-held beliefs. We believe that you aren't truly learning until you're made a little uncomfortable or have your ideas challenged. In the end, you might not only learn something yourself but also discover a book that you can recommend to someone else in their time of need. To that end, you can find a list of our recommendations in the appendix of this book.

Reading is important work, and it's work we have to make time for. Why? Because leaders read.

LEADERS' REFLECTION QUESTIONS:

1. How did leadership character become cultivated in you in your life? Can you think of specific people who influenced it?
2. What book changed your perspective on reading? What touched you about that book?

> Share on social media how your students are showing good character and/or reading diverse books that support the development of their character. Use the hashtag #WhenKidsLead.

PART
2

STUDENT JOBS

A leader is someone who is responsible and takes charge.
Leaders ensure that all the duties asked of them and their
team are completed with excellence, and do so with diligence
while setting a good example for those around them.

—HUNTER, AGE 18

In part 1, we shared why we believe youth leadership training is critical for a stronger society and how this training can be done. As we continue, we dive deeper into when and where adults can inspire, empower, and grow leadership in our children.

First, we must recognize that educators possess a powerful gift in their hand. It is the offering of student empowerment. Unfortunately, we often do not present the gift because of fear of failure, discomfort, relinquished control, or change. But for our students to become leaders, we educators must empower them with opportunity. Over the next few chapters, we share those opportunities in the form of student jobs which, if done correctly, will cultivate responsibility, integrity, creativity, and courage in our students.

Keep in mind that our examples are just a slice of the pie. Your ability to extend leadership opportunities should travel in many directions and down many avenues. Students' taking on roles and responsibilities looks different in each school and varies depending on needs, structures, and the adults involved. We implore that when you create these opportunities for your students, you keep in mind that all students deserve a chance, no matter their background or story.

And it matters what you call these jobs. As Eric Jensen observed in his book *Engaging Students with Poverty in Mind*, "Many job titles in the elementary classroom are, if not entirely meaningless, the epitome of low expectations: a pencil sharpener, a light monitor, a caboose. Have you ever had a student tell you, 'I want to be a line leader when I grow up'?" He goes on to explain that by upgrading these classroom jobs to real-world positions, such as mechanic, electrician, and tour guide, we are giving our students a chance to "set goals and dreams in an authentic context."

For example, Ms. Hawk, Ryder's first-grade teacher, applied Jensen's approach for her classroom jobs. One day Ryder came home from school so excited that he was the class electrician, explaining that he is in charge of turning on and off the lights for the class. He learned from Ms. Hawk about the role of an electrician in society and how they are important to our day-to-day living. She built up the authentic context of this profession enough that it made Ryder even more excited about the job. If you implement a system like this in your classroom, creating a framework around each job and building real-world aspirations around it increase the students' enthusiasm and lead to more effective leadership training.

When providing students with real-world titles for classroom jobs, it is also appropriate to have real-world expectations, such as their showing up and doing their job to the best of their ability. Most employers would agree that these are the minimum requirements to keep a job. So in your classroom, to get or maintain a job, students need to be at school and consistently do their job well. The natural consequence for not doing the minimum would be to lose the job.

By the same token, when students exceed job-related expectations, they should be recognized by others. Our concluding chapter explores ways to celebrate leaders and recognize the important contributions they bring to our classrooms.

3

GREETER

A leader is someone who steps up and takes charge. It's a person who isn't afraid to take initiative and doesn't follow the crowd. A leader is someone who stands up for everyone.

—LANDON, AGE 12

If you ever had the pleasure of walking into a kindergarten classroom, you likely experienced what we like to call "the bee swarm." Kindergartners are known for their love and admiration of everyone (and everything) they encounter, and this is frequently demonstrated through hugs. Imagine all these littles surrounding you at once, much like a swarm of bees. Unlike the sting of bees, however, you instead receive embraces that can't help but make you smile. Still, while a swarm of kindergartners is sweet and cute, it is not good classroom practice to have an entire class greet a person. It can be disruptive to classroom instruction and a little alarming to any classroom guest. By having an assigned classroom greeter, the interruption can be avoided and the person who enters the classroom can feel welcomed but not overwhelmed.

This warm, comfortable feeling of being welcomed is something that can and should be extended from every classroom, no matter the age. While swarms of hugs may be less likely in classrooms above the kindergarten level, the idea of making people feel welcome when they walk into a classroom is quite feasible.

ADAM

When I became principal at Moore Magnet Elementary, I established a school-wide expectation that each classroom would have a greeter to welcome any adult who entered. For example, we frequently hosted perspective parents to determine if they would like to send their child to our school. During the tour, when we walked into a classroom, the greeter would walk over to the parent and me, shake hands with each of us, say "Good morning, Mr. Dovico" (since they already knew me), and then proceed to greet the parent. The greeting consisted of the child introducing himself or herself, sharing what learning was taking place at that moment in the classroom, and then inviting the guest to join if they wished. It might have gone something like this: "Good morning. My name is Ethan. Welcome to Ms. Parker's second grade class. Right now we're in guided reading groups. Please feel free to join us. It was nice to meet you."

The greeter never has to ask permission to be excused from their learning activity when a visitor arrives and is expected to be stealthy in getting to the guest so as not to disrupt classmates or instruction. Additionally, it is understood that the other students in the classroom are to continue their work and let the greeter do his or her job.

Even if not entering a classroom, every visitor should be warmly greeted. Therefore, in addition to the classroom greeter, each classroom was expected to have a hallway greeter. The purpose of the hallway greeter was to ensure that adults in the building are seen and welcomed. Too often, guests walk down a school hallway never acknowledged. We have both visited many schools across the country, and it can be horribly uncomfortable walking into a place where you are essentially invisible. There is something about being acknowledged when you are in a new place that makes you feel much more at ease. This is where the hallway greeter comes in.

If a lined-up class walking down the hallway spots an adult in the hall, the hallway greeter breaks the line, approaches the adult, and shakes hands with and greets the adult. If it was someone they were familiar with, such as another teacher, the greeter might say, "Good morning, Mr. Hicks. I hope you're having a good day." If the adult is a guest in the school, the greeter might say, "Good morning. My name is Jacob. Welcome to Moore Elementary. What brings you to our school today?" After the greeting is complete, he or she would return to the line. This is also an excellent lesson in the importance of learning everyone's name.

As a school who is growing leaders, help your students learn the names of every adult on campus—the maintenance workers, custodial staff, cafeteria workers, front office staff, and everyone in between. It shows that *everyone* in the school holds value and deserves respect. And on a side note, it is just as important for the adults in the building to know the kids' names!

No matter the location of the greeting, the purpose remains the same: welcome people into our school and make sure they are "seen." As principals, we wanted to make sure that every person who walks into our buildings felt comfortable and was treated like part of the family.

HOW TO TRAIN GREETERS

One option to train greeters is to utilize the SPECIAL system described in the opening chapter. Building student leadership is about providing students these and related tools (e.g., how to give a firm handshake and how to hold a conversation) to keep in their back pocket so that when an unfamiliar or high-stakes situation presents itself, they can retrieve and use those tools to be successful in navigating it. Several of those elements are actually fundamental to being a successful greeter.

SHAKING HANDS

Greeters will almost always start their job with an extension of their hand. Most adults do not expect a child to extend a hand to shake, so this may catch adults off guard or take them a moment to realize the child's intention. Teach students to keep their hand extended until the adult responds with a handshake or a verbal or body cue that they would not like to shake hands. Children also need to understand that their strength is different than an adult's, so what might feel to a child as squeezing too hard may actually be an appropriate amount of force to shake an adult's hand. Remember to provide immediate feedback when practicing so that students conceptualize what a firm handshake feels like.

EYE CONTACT

Students can practice maintaining eye contact with a speaker throughout their day. In the classroom, encourage students to look at the speaker, whether a teacher or classmate. This practice will reinforce the habit when it comes to greeting. While training greeters, it is important to differentiate between staring and good eye contact. Maintaining good eye contact does not mean looking at the speaker during every second of interaction. The eyes naturally need to refocus at times. Inform students that this exercise is more about ensuring that the other person knows that they have the greeter's attention.

CHARM

An effective greeter comes off as natural and relatable. Interacting with someone who laughs at their jokes, nods in agreement, and smiles upon seeing them is desirable for all guests. While your youngest greeters may not understand the proper timing to show some of these elements, leading with a warm smile is a great start. From there, older students can add these other traits as they develop awareness about reading cues. To teach students these skills, model the different stories that a face can tell simply by exhibiting different expressions. Remind your greeters that people read their body language as well, so the facial expressions or body posture they make will translate to how a person perceives them.

ASKING A QUESTION

People like to talk about themselves. It's natural. One part of a greeter's job is to engage people in discussing things about themselves. While some situations may require specific content knowledge or field-specific questioning, an array of questions would certainly make for a good casual conversation. Empower your greeters to rise to the challenge of knowing what to ask by providing some examples:

- Do you have a favorite place you have visited?
- Do you play any sports or have any hobbies?
- Tell me about your family.
- What's the nicest thing someone has done for you?
- What are your memories of elementary/middle/high school?
- Tell me about where you grew up.
- What's your favorite movie?

- Do you have a favorite food?
- What was your favorite television show growing up?

Greeters often think they need to ask an entire list of questions such as these. Teach the trainees that asking one question will likely be enough, because if they do a good job of listening (the *L* in SPECIAL), they can take someone's response and turn it into another question. Modeling this for students and then having them break down what you did is typically most effective. It might go something like this:

Greeter: Hi! My name is Adam. What's your name?

Guest: Hi. I'm Todd.

Greeter: It's nice to meet you. How are you today?

Guest: I'm doing well. How about yourself?

Greeter: I'm doing great. Thank you for asking. I'd love to learn more about you. Do you have any favorite memories of when you were in fifth grade?

Guest: I remember going on a field trip to Washington, D. C., in fifth grade.

Greeter: That must have been so much fun! Do you remember what you saw when you were there?

Guest: We saw the Capitol Building, the White House, and the Lincoln Memorial.

Greeter: That sounds amazing. I hope I get to go there one day too. Thanks for sharing a little bit about yourself. I hope you have a great visit to our school. It was a pleasure meeting you!

Obviously, the execution of a conversation like this can go many different ways. And the last thing you want is your greeter to come off sounding like a robot, so allow your greeters to be natural and word their dialogue the way that they feel comfortable.

At this point you may feel overwhelmed with the number of layers involved with training greeters. Remember that a great place to begin is by starting simple. You don't have to jump completely into applying a system such as SPECIAL right away. Look at the kids you have in front of you to decide what you feel is most important for them to learn. It might be that eye contact is a huge issue for you this year and so you really want them to focus on that concept. You might find that the art and science of the handshake is a great place to start. Whatever that starting point is for you, remember that teaching these foundational skills leads to building many of the leadership skills and character traits that we focus on in this book.

GREETERS FAQ

We frequently present on this topic in schools across the country to help them implement this practice, and there are a few questions that pop up frequently that you might have as well.

WHY IS LEARNING TO BE A GREETER IMPORTANT?

Sometimes we are asked why anyone would spend time teaching skills such as the ones we've listed above, especially to our youngest kids. It's our belief that students will have the most opportunities and the best chance to be successful if they are as prepared as possible. It also never hurts to make a positive impression! Whether it's meeting your teacher for the first time, introducing yourself to a coach, meeting a notable figure or your new neighbor, or just looking to stand out from the crowd, these skills are innumerable in application and lasting in purpose.

But there's more value to being a greeter than just making a good first impression on someone else. Students are developing courage by approaching adults and typically being the first to extend their hand to shake. They are building empathy and kindness by asking questions of individuals they meet and listening intently to their stories, especially when no one else might care to ask. And they are building responsibility by executing their classroom job to the best of their ability and representing their classroom and school.

WHEN DO I DO THE TRAINING?

This depends on whether greeters are a job solely in your classroom or throughout the school. If greeters are being implemented throughout the school, the skills, procedures, and expectations should be presented in an assembly-style setting so that all stakeholders hear a single message. This type of training is best done at the beginning of the school year when routines and procedures are being put into place. If the greeter job covers only your classroom, training should be done also as early on in the school year as possible, when other classroom jobs and routines are explained. Additional training can then subsequently take place in small pockets of time before or after school, at recess, during advisory or homeroom time, or during natural settings such as when students are entering or exiting the classroom or school.

Remember, not all skills need to be delivered in one sitting. It is best to introduce the skills at an age-appropriate pace over a period of time. For Adam, his initial training usually took place over three or four forty-five-minute sessions. From there, he conducted minisessions of about five to ten minutes each to reinforce old or introduce new skills.

HOW LONG DOES A GREETER KEEP THE JOB?

While we leave this decision up to teachers, we have found that three to four weeks was a good duration for a greeter to have the job. This period of time enabled the student to get used to the position and have ample opportunities to practice but still allowed several students to hold the position.

WHAT HAPPENS IF THE GREETER IS ABSENT OR OUT OF THE ROOM?

Each classroom would have at least one backup greeter who would be on standby at all times. The backup greeter is also a great way to have a "next in line" for the rotation of the greeter job.

WHAT DO YOU DO ABOUT THE STUDENT WHO ALWAYS WANTS TO BE THE GREETER?

The success of the greeter job comes with clear expectations and routines. Like any classroom job, it must be shared. Indeed, part of being a good leader is letting others lead (see chapter 11).

DOES EVERY KID NEED TO BE A GREETER?

Forcing kids into leadership roles when they don't feel ready doesn't make much sense. There are many ways to build students as leaders, and being a greeter is only one of them. Indeed, this book is all about identifying the many different leadership opportunities that exist. Finding a good fit between the student and task is a major part of the leadership role as a teacher.

Not every child will want to or need to be a greeter, but please never deny a child who wants to be a greeter simply because you think that child is incapable of doing it. You will be pleasantly surprised at who emerges as your strongest greeters. It might not be who you expect!

CAN I HAVE GREETERS IN MIDDLE OR HIGH SCHOOL?

We believe that this program is even more important in middle and high school! These are real-life skills, and students in these grade levels are of an age when they should be beginning to refine them. If we're truly preparing our students to be successful in the world, we need to help them develop soft skills as well as academic skills.

While the classroom greeter position would look the same, the hallway greeter may differ since most middle and high school classes do not walk together through the halls. Therefore, we suggest that you assign a group of students to be school-wide hallway greeters. A one-to-fifty ratio should give you enough greeters for a school, so if you have a school population of nine hundred students, eighteen to twenty greeters should cover the grounds.

DOES HAVING GREETERS REALLY MAKE A DIFFERENCE?

Todd saw a tremendous difference at his campus when they implemented classroom greeters. We received countless comments from guests (especially central office visitors) who were impressed with our inviting, well-spoken, and knowledgeable students.

Not only did it give students more ownership of their classroom but using SPECIAL helped teachers train students practically in how to speak with and greet others. In fact, our oldest students on campus, who were trained first, then acted as leaders to teach our youngest ones. They loved being trusted enough to teach the importance of a warm greeting to our littles on campus, and it provided another opportunity for them to build relationships with all the students.

CONCLUSION

Our hope is that students are able to use these skills in everyday life—patronizing a restaurant, applying for jobs, meeting new people, and so on. We live in a world now where a strong grade point average and a solid transcript aren't the only qualifications employers are looking for, so it begs the question, what will help a young leader stand out? We believe that making a great first impression will certainly help, and when we are able to not only teach the skills necessary to do so but also encourage students to apply these skills in their own lives, we are giving them a leg up in a competitive world. When our youth feel more confident in who they are and what they bring to the table, this self-belief will translate over to that job interview.

Classroom and hallway greeters transformed the way people were welcomed into our schools. At the end of their visit, guests of the school often referenced their exchanges with greeters. Many parents would tell us that their children wanted to do this classroom job most. But more than transforming the way we welcomed people into our school, the role transformed our students. We witnessed numerous students who used to run away when adults said hello blossoming into confident children by serving in this role.

TODD

As the building principal, my favorite part about adding the greeters was the look of surprise and amazement by different adults when they would come and visit the campus.

It's something special when a six-year-old can greet you at the door and hold an entire conversation with you and invite you into the learning space. It sends a powerful message, no matter if it's central office, an adult enrolling their child, a visiting parent, or even the mayor!

When the mayor did stop by our campus one day to read a story to a classroom, he dropped by my office on the way out just to let me know that he was so impressed with the way the second grade classroom greeter welcomed him. He let me know that he was going to send several of his staff to our campus to witness the way our students greeted adults as they enter a room so that his staff could learn some great pointers!

ADAM

One day, I got a call from the head of human resources for the school district. He said that the local news station was doing a story on our district's upcoming teacher recruitment fair and they needed a school setting to film the news story. I agreed, and that afternoon a few central office folks met the news station at my school.

While there, the news anchor and the cameraman were getting B-roll footage to show as a part of the story on the recruitment fair. As I walked the anchor and cameraman down the hallway to a few classes, they were greeted several times by hallway and then classroom greeters as we entered rooms. They were so blown away by their experience that they asked if they could come back and do a story on our greeters.

They did come back and create a great piece. After the video was posted on social media, it ended up going viral and received 1.5 million views on Facebook. I received messages from people all over the world asking about this program and was encouraged to hear from people who implemented this practice in their school. The more students who have the opportunity to build and refine these leadership skills at an early age, the stronger our future will be when they are adults. It's never too early to prepare for what's ahead.

LEADERS' REFLECTION QUESTIONS:

1. How can you leverage support from stakeholders in and around your school campus to get a program like greeters off the ground? Are there individuals or groups who could provide additional training or resources?

2. What specific training do you need to execute with your students to make them effective greeters? When and where would you do it?

Share your classroom or hallway greeters program
in action using the hashtag #WhenKidsLead.

4

AMBASSADORS

A leader is someone who sets a good example for others, helps their team through anything whenever help is needed, gives them great morale, and never gives up.

—CHASE, AGE 16

A s with any program or activity, you will have certain students who shine, those who are naturally gifted or who work tremendously hard to become standouts. While Adam's classroom and hallway greeter program was a powerful way to engage the larger student population into learning and practicing basic greeting skills, he wanted to raise the bar and give further opportunities to those who excelled with social interactions. To recognize and train those students who desired to take greeting to another level, Adam created the Ambassador program.

ADAM

I'll never forget the first "gig" that my inaugural Ambassador team took on. I organized a community gathering at the school, to which I invited local business owners and employees to join in. As a new principal, I wanted to build relationships with the community, and inviting them to attend our event was an easy way to do that. Many of them passed by the school every day on the way to work but had never been inside.

The day finally arrived, and the kids were so excited. As each community member entered, an Ambassador greeted the individual and then welcomed them for a tour of the school. As the groups toured, I observed so many of the strategies that we had practiced—walking backwards to address multiple people, employing strong eye contact and hand motions, using visual cues around the building to remember stories, and questioning mindfully to learn more about each individual's life.

I was so proud of the team. They represented the school and themselves flawlessly. I could see their pride as they left an impression on the community members who visited. In fact, a number of the community members ended up becoming school partners because of their visit, attributing their desire to do so from their encounter with the Ambassadors.

My Ambassadors did much more than just conduct tours. When we had community events, such as a neighborhood gathering where local schools each had a table, they joined and talked with families who came up to our ours. We chose to create an interactive booth, so the Ambassadors ran engaging activities and talked with our visitors as they learned more about our school. The students would explain who they were and then ask families if they would like to come over to the school for a tour one day. A number of families who later enrolled in our school said that it was their

Ambassadors Eliana and Ve'Nise deliver an impromptu
speech at a teacher appreciation event.

conversation with an Ambassador that convinced them to send
their child to our school. They were our own best salespeople!

Ambassadors also talked to potential teachers for open positions
during the school district's annual teacher recruitment fairs. In
fact, after meeting someone, the kids would often come up to me
and share their thoughts! A few Ambassadors even came up with
little signals to communicate to me whether I needed to speak to

a person or not. Kids have great intuition. And on a side note, if you want to truly leverage student leadership, include a student on your interview committee for new hires!

Finally, a few select Ambassadors would even join us on stage at times and speak to large crowds. They learned to expect the unexpected because we would hand over the microphone and they would have to deliver a speech. Once, two of my star Ambassadors, Eliana and Ve'Nise, served at a teacher appreciation event and the superintendent unexpectedly asked them to deliver a thank-you message to the teachers in attendance. They were handed the mic, and they delivered! It was an important lesson that day for the two girls to realize that even though you are not always mentally prepared for something, you can still shine when you are equipped with the right skills.

CHOOSING AMBASSADORS

In determining which students are eligible to be an Ambassador, first decide what grade levels you would like to include in this program. In elementary school, we suggest using your oldest grade, as they are likely to be more confident as the oldest kids in the school. In middle and high school, it is less important what grades you use since students in each of those grades would have the skill sets necessary to be successful.

To become an Ambassador at Adam's school there were several steps involved.

1. Participants had to be in fifth grade. This grade was his oldest students, and he wanted something for younger students to look forward to at the end of their elementary career.

2. Students needed to complete the application by the deadline. The application required their homeroom teacher's signature and the signatures of three specialists, such as an art, music, or physical education teacher, or a librarian. This requirement helped to ensure that students behaved responsibly throughout the school, not only in their homeroom. The application also included an essay section that asked them to answer this question: "Why do you want to be an Ambassador?"

3. Those students who successfully completed the application were eligible to sit down for an interview with Adam's assistant principal, instructional coach, school counselor, and himself. During the interview, they asked a series of questions that challenged the students' knowledge of the school and them. The interviewers weren't concerned as much about the content of the answer as they were about the students' ability to think quickly on their feet and be charming and sensible in their response.

4. The final stage was a mock tour that each student gave to the judges. During the exercise, the students had the length of the hallway, or about 30 seconds, to talk about the school and highlight what they thought were the most important elements. Again, the team wasn't as much concerned about the content as their ability to be natural and engaging.

On average, approximately thirty to forty students would try out. Adam would select around five or six for the initial team of Ambassadors. Later in the year, he would typically carry out another round to add a few more.

TODD

The Ambassador program at my campus was managed a little differently to fit our school's needs. I had about 120 fifth graders and really wanted to grow them in these skills. I always spent quite a bit of time with my students at lunch, recess, and PE to really get to know them outside of the educational setting and to see more of their personalities.

Each year, I would talk with our fifth graders in the cafeteria about being an Ambassador and giving tours. I would really build the program up to increase their excitement and anticipation. After spending this time talking about it, I would take volunteers right there on the spot. Now keep in mind I wasn't limiting myself only to these volunteers. Before even going into the cafeteria to select participants, I had already spoken with students' teachers about recommendations, and I had already decided on my own too. Sometimes a child can't see their own leadership qualities quite yet and they need an adult who will come alongside and mentor them. So on that day at lunch after choosing a few of the volunteers, I would also call a few names of students that their teachers or I had preselected.

Regardless of how you choose Ambassadors, we both agree it has been a fantastic journey watching students take on that leadership role. And what we can affirm is that the students who sometimes give you the most trouble are the ones who end up making the best Ambassadors. It just takes someone believing in them.

HOW TO TRAIN AMBASSADORS

Dedicated training for your Ambassadors is essential to the success of the program. While many students have the potential to be excellent at the job, without the proper preparation, they will be a deer in headlights the first time they come face-to-face with a task. Questions abound, from who will do the training to when it will happen.

ADAM

At my school, the selected team of Ambassadors received an intense boot camp training from me over the course of several weeks. During this time, we reviewed the foundational greeting behaviors (which most of them were already good at). I then introduced telling the story, asking follow-up questions based on what people said, differentiating conversations, addressing small and large groups, giving tours, identifying specific areas of the school, walking backwards, keeping a group moving, closing out a conversation, and so on.

To train students on most of these skills, we brought the discussion back to SPECIAL to begin. For example, when teaching storytelling, I emphasized the importance of using facial expressions, body language, speaking posture, and eye contact to connect to listeners. But I also introduced new concepts to students, such as voice cadence, pitch, and tone, which add to the impact of a story.

When teaching about addressing a small group (usually less than five) versus a large group, you begin by reminding the student about eye contact but then add in that as a group gets larger, eye contact becomes more about "connect and move on" instead of sticking with one or two people to connect with. Also, as a group gets larger, students may not be able to shake everyone's hand because it will take up too much time. This is where you teach students sporadic handshaking, where they transition to shaking the hand of every third or fourth person to ensure that people are not standing in line waiting for their handshake.

One of the most challenging skills to teach is how to naturally close out a conversation. Many kids end a conversation by simply stopping talking. Instead, Ambassadors should be taught how to recognize when a conversation needs to end (because of a time constraint or a lack of things to talk about). They then extend their hand and say something like "It was a pleasure meeting you today. I hope you have a fantastic visit." That's typically a universally accepted message that the conversation has come to an end.

Much like training greeters, Ambassador training is best done through modeling, immediate feedback, and real-life scenarios and role-play.

It might sound like a lot, and it was, but the students absolutely loved it. They understood that this was a highly coveted position, and if they wanted to remain on the team, they had to work for it. As with being a greeter, students were building the leadership traits courage (addressing new faces and large crowds), responsibility (representing the school), kindness (making someone's day better), and empathy (listening to others' stories and understanding who the speakers are).

As you can see from our stories on implementing Ambassador programs at our schools, there are multiple ways that you can prepare your students for the job. The same can be said for finding the time to train your students in being an Ambassador. Think of times in the day when you can pull the group together. If you are a classroom teacher looking to implement an Ambassador program, look for small chunks of time at recess, lunch, before or after school, or during a study hall period to conduct your training. Even three- to five-minute minisessions could be sufficient to practice a specific skill. It may also be helpful to identify additional staff throughout the school who can assist you with the training or fill in for you when you are not available. School counselors, career or life skills teachers, coaches, or administrators may be willing to assist in your training program, if you provide specific needs and tasks to work on.

CONCLUSION

If you are contemplating starting an Ambassador program, consider the needs of the school and where the Ambassadors might fit. Perhaps it is in providing tours to community members and potential families. Maybe it is serving at community events and school functions. Think of any opportunities where a young leader may be an added asset to the school personnel that typically attend these functions. In these cases, it is important for others to know that the Ambassador holds a special role in the school. Consider a special shirt, badge, pin, sash, tie, jacket, or emblem that the Ambassador can sport while in the role.

Providing opportunities to implement the Ambassador skills being taught is vital if students are going to see this training as valuable. We recommend finding ways to invite visitors to the school as frequently as possible for practice so that students stay fresh on their feet. When Adam was conducting training for my students in the front lobby of my school, he would often grab a parent volunteering in the front office to be a guinea pig for the Ambassadors to test their new skills on. The parents absolutely loved it and were always willing to give a helping hand.

The truest compliment to the credibility of a system is when it is used with no one watching over it. While the implementation of an Ambassador system makes for a great visual inside the school and serves as a talking point for families or community members when experienced at an event or gathering, we are most proud when our Ambassadors represented themselves without us being present.

ADAM

One of my Ambassadors, DJ, was at a local park with his sister on a Saturday. DJ saw a student he recognized from school and knew was new this year. DJ took it upon himself to go up to the father of the boy, shake his hand, and introduce himself. He said, "Hi. My name is DJ, and I'm a fifth grader at Moore. We're so happy to have Hank at our school this year."

Those few words almost brought the father to tears. The father knew that DJ didn't have to say anything to him, that a ten-year-old playing on the playground is having far more fun playing than going up to a stranger and introducing himself. But DJ had also been taught as an Ambassador that the job is twenty-four seven and that you never know who you can impact and how your words and actions can change someone's day. DJ certainly made this father's day and was the epitome of what we value in our Ambassadors.

Naturally, the hope is that any student would do what DJ did. But we also know that not every student is ready for that leap. We need to differentiate training and make sure that we are building each student to eventually get to that comfort level, but we also need to understand that it's important to meet students where they are. Luckily, every school does have a DJ who is ready to be held to the highest expectations and use their Ambassador skills wherever they go.

After hearing all that has gone into our Ambassador programs, it may scare you a bit to start a program of your own. Please know that it can be whatever you like it to be. It shouldn't be an intimidating endeavor, but it is certainly one that requires dedication. In the end, no matter how you design the program, by implementing a program you are showing the school, families, and community that you value face-to-face interactions and the power that they can have on preparing our students for successful futures. The students are going to take it only as seriously as the adults behind it. So if you are dedicated, motivated, and supported, go for it!

LEADERS' REFLECTION QUESTIONS:

1. What roles could Ambassadors play at your school? Where could they best serve the needs that exist?
2. How would you formulate a selection process for your Ambassador program? Who would be involved, and what criteria is important to you?

> Share why you believe programs like student ambassadors are important to have in place at a school and how it prepares students for the future using the hashtag #WhenKidsLead.

5

SOCIAL MEDIA INTERNS

A leader is someone who always encourages others to be the best they can be. They also always hold themselves to high standards yet remain understanding and accepting of others. A leader doesn't always realize they are a leader. They just use their talents to bless and inspire others. They don't let negativity distract them from focusing on their goals.

—MACY, AGE 16

Both of us have experienced how social media has transformed not only our professional lives but also our personal ones. Our eyes have been opened to the fire-hydrant flow of information and learning that can take place when we put ourselves out there on platforms such as Twitter, Instagram, Facebook, and YouTube, just to name a few. We've also seen the ugly side of social media. We've seen the bullying, the mean comments people can throw from the safety of their bedroom behind their screen, the crazy things people write.

Our kids have access to more technology and social media than we could have ever dreamed. They're also bombarded with social media messages that don't always come from reliable sources or are used in demeaning ways. The more we can help kids see the power of social media for good, the more likely they will become leaders who use it to instigate change and make a positive impact. That's why we wanted to address the importance of social media in growing student leaders.

If you've watched the news in recent years, you've seen time and time again that kids are rising up to stand against injustice by using social media to unify and amplify their messaging. From young leaders like David Hogg from Marjory Stoneman Douglas High School in Parkland, Florida, speaking out against gun violence to Greta Thunberg of Sweden educating people about climate change, social media in the hands of youth is a mechanism for encouraging people to take action. But students don't have to be at the forefront of a movement to be a leader; they can learn how to use social media to help their school and develop important leadership qualities along the way.

STARTING SMALL AT SCHOOL

As campus leaders, we were both adamant about making sure that we told our own stories. We didn't want anyone outside of our campus telling an incomplete story of our classrooms, our students, or our school. All it takes is one angry parent or community member to share a negative story about your school or district, and then it becomes the narrative. By being the author of your own story, that one angry individual becomes the anomaly, not the headline.

TODD

When I became principal of a school in Navasota, Texas, everything was new to me and I had so much to learn. What I quickly came to realize was how the perceptions of parents (or the public at large) can begin to define the way a campus is viewed by all. I knew exactly how hard my team and I were working, the things that were being accomplished, the mountains that were being moved. But that one negative Facebook post or Instagram message would always break us down as a school. We wanted others to see and value our hard work, too!

So I started using my social media platform to tell the story of my school. I knew that people tend to get their news from various places, so I created school accounts with Twitter, Snapchat, Instagram, Remind, Periscope, and Facebook. I wanted to meet as many families as I could when they were online. Why? Because when someone shares something negative about a school or district online, where is the first place people go? They go to that organization's Facebook page or website. And if your website or page hasn't been updated in weeks (besides for upcoming events), visitors may judge that organization as less than credible.

I began with a mission to share a minimum of five photos every day on our social media platforms. I believe that a picture really is worth a thousand words, and I knew those photos could speak more about the work of our campus than anything else.

When this all began, I was the only one sharing our story. I would use our school hashtag and share photos of the great work happening on campus every day. Slowly I began to see the perception of our school change. But still I knew it wasn't enough. My perspective on the great things happening on campus couldn't be the only perspective shared.

My next step was getting the staff involved in sharing the story of our school. I wanted them to take ownership as well. Plus, inviting them to share took a load off me as the sole voice. We held trainings over how to use social media, offered incentives, and built capacity. Everyone learns at different levels and speeds, so I was careful not to push anyone too hard but to push nonetheless. I wanted my team to understand the importance of this work and how, once it became a natural part of their day, it would become easier.

I remember hearing about the idea of "social media interns" and I immediately fell in love with the idea and knew I had to bring this concept back to my campus. This was the missing piece! I had spent so much time valuing and amplifying the voices of the adults on campus that I had forgotten just how important the voices and perspectives of our students are as well.

THE JOB OF SOCIAL MEDIA INTERN

Now before we go any further, let's be sure to clarify something. There are age-limit laws for creating social media accounts for children under thirteen. At no point should any adult sit down with kids and help them create their own accounts. We made sure our students were using our school accounts (after all, that is the point) and devices that were previously logged into (so we didn't share passwords with them). But we can't as educators sit back and expect parents and other leaders in our society to solely set the example for being a good digital citizen. We know the importance of teaching kids how powerful their words are—especially on social media. It's imperative that we invest time teaching our students how to use social media responsibly.

So I began my own version of employing social media interns at Webb Elementary. I decided to start with my fifth graders on campus, as they were the oldest students at my school, hoping that what they found great about our school would be different than what we as adults were choosing to advertise. As the project began to take off, I watched a more robust image of our school materialize, a story that highlighted the great work from all the angles of the campus. More personal stories and insights into our school were being shared, and we were squarely in charge of our own narrative.

The process I used was to "hire" two fifth graders for a three-week cycle, with specific tasks defined and learning curves accounted for. Here's how the process worked:

WEEK ONE:

This first week was all about trial and error. The week began with my two new interns stopping by my office daily. When they arrived, I would send them with an iPad to take ten photos around campus. This was a test, of course, to see how good their photography skills were. As we all know, a child doesn't necessarily take the most flattering pictures; you have to teach them to avoid taking photos that include kids picking their nose or students bent over their desks doing work sheets (an inevitable part of education but something we do not necessarily want to publicize). I wanted to see how strong their natural photography instincts were before I tried to give them any direction on how to take photos.

Throughout this process, I also had constant conversations and brainstorming sessions with the students about how they could make sure they did not interrupt classroom instruction while taking photos. We never wanted the classroom teachers to feel like the social media interns were in the way or disrupting the environment.

These lessons are not natural for many of our students. There were times when I as the adult had to go into classrooms with some interns to model for them ways to take photos without being a nuisance. But before reaching that point, the students were always given an opportunity to show their skills at photography first.

We also talked extensively about what we wanted our message to be and how we wanted to portray ourselves to the community. Many times, especially younger students, they don't realize how their words or actions are coming across to adults. So before posting photos that first week we would have in-depth conversations about what message they thought each photo was sending, why that message was important, and how other people might interpret that photo's message.

Once the students crafted the message, they would end it with the hashtag #KidTweet along with our school hashtag. We discussed how to post photos, the importance of staff members' names, students who couldn't be photographed, and what we wanted the messages to be. It was always fun to listen to their perspectives and their insight on what should be highlighted.

A word to the wise: If you are active on several social media platforms, don't feel like you always have to post to all of them to keep up. You'll drive yourself crazy. So many great productivity tools are out there to help you post in multiple places at once. A favorite of ours is IFTTT. It allows you to create "recipes" where a singular post easily ends up on all your social media platforms in one click!

WEEK TWO:

After a week of letting the two interns experiment and learn under my watchful eye, I let them loose in week two. During this week, my two interns don't have to check in with me at all. Each day, they come down to my office and grab my iPad from where they know it is kept. They take about ten to fifteen minutes to move around campus and snap photos. They then create their own social media posts, return the iPad, and head back to class. They do all this never having to speak a word to me. (I, of course, check in on the hashtag each day and check out their posts, providing feedback only as necessary.)

I am hands-off purposefully in this second week because I want them to see that I trust them. When you show students you trust them but at the same time set clear expectations, they catch you by surprise again and again. They learn that their voice truly does matter and that they don't have to only regurgitate what the adults have told them. They also begin to understand the power of their voice, that they exert influence and can shape the perception of the environment in which they reside. When kids begin to not only be told their voice matters but actually believe it, that's when they begin to internalize the idea that they can use their voice, and social media, for good.

WEEK THREE:

On Monday of their third week, they sit down for a meeting with me. At this meeting they let me know the two new interns they think would make good replacements. During this conversation, I either agree with their choices or gently suggest alternatives.

Don't be afraid to take risks with some of your student leadership choices. Pick the students who might not first come to mind, especially those students who can cause discipline issues. They are the ones who need leadership opportunities and avenues so they can see how great it feels when they make good choices. You might be surprised at how much children bloom when they finally hear that someone believes in and trusts them.

After we've decided on the two new interns, my current interns make their way down the hallway to inform the new hires of their selection. They then spend the rest of their third week training the newbies.

CONCLUSION

Author Stephen Covey says, "I am not a product of my circumstances. I am a product of my decisions." If we wait around while others explain our story for us, we will become a product of circumstance. That product is uncontrolled, unpredictable, and can negatively impact many facets of your school. Instead, we want you to decide to be proactive and swim to the ship instead of waiting for it to come to the dock. Take charge of your classroom or school narrative. Use images to share the inspiring things you and your students are doing by allowing your kids to lead by presenting the world through their eyes.

Although Todd had social media interns for four years, after that first week of training in year one, he never had to train kids again. They took over the training of their peers and did a far more thorough job than he ever had. And, again, they felt empowered to lead!

By amplifying the voices of not only our staff but also our students, we watched the involvement in and responses to our social media messages grow exponentially. If you want parents involved with what you're sharing online, empower students. Some school districts in Texas allow high school seniors to manage the websites and social media for the entire district!

When we relinquish a little control and find ways to empower our kids, we will continually be blown away by how they choose to lead. So today we encourage you to strategically and mindfully let go, give your kids more control, and imagine the possibilities.

LEADERS' REFLECTION QUESTIONS:

1. What fear do you have of using social media interns at your school? How can you work to educate yourself more on the power that lies in telling your story and connecting with others?

2. Understanding that all adults (and children) learn at different levels, how could you introduce the power of telling your story through the eyes of kids to fellow teachers or administrators on campus or in the district?

Share on social media your school's story through the eyes of the students. Use the hashtag #WhenKidsLead.

PART
3

STUDENT VOICES

A leader is one who leads people, protects them, and guides them to greatness!

—AUDREY, AGE 9

Leadership opportunities originate and evolve from a wide variety of needs and desires. Think about your own life. A managerial position opens up for a new project, your kid's baseball team needs a coach, the church asks you to lead a ministry, you decide to start volunteering in your community. And when it comes down to it, adults generally feel comfortable envisioning students serving, or at least training to serve, in real-life leadership roles in which we similarly perform.

In the first half of the book, we presented scenarios in which you can visualize students performing real-life roles such as greeter, ambassador, and social media intern. Examining these roles deeper, you will find that adults are ultimately the drivers of kids' leading. Adults are establishing roles, selecting or rotating participants, explicitly training and guiding, and facilitating directions in which the leadership may turn. There's nothing wrong with that involvement, and it is a great place to start as you begin or continue your journey on empowering kids to lead.

We will now transition to identifying opportunities for the voices and minds of students to shine apart from leadership roles identified by adults. Ahead, you will read examples of ways that we have facilitated or witnessed student expression, choice, and collaboration in the process of cultivating leadership. While the stories and models will offer ideas to bring to your children, we encourage you to continue brainstorming beyond this list to uncover further ways that student voice can inspire leadership.

6

SPEECHES

*A leader is someone people follow
because they look up to them.*

—GRANT, AGE 10

ADAM

In June of 1994 at Demarest Elementary School in Bloomfield, New Jersey, I stood in front of my classmates and our families as a sixth grader at our "graduation" from elementary school. I had been selected by my peers as one of the four students from our class to speak at the event. My three classmates and I had been assigned parts throughout the ceremony when we spoke about our memories in elementary school and forecasted what the future would hold.

I had practiced a thousand times, and I even had the script in front of me on the podium. But to my memory, it was the first time I had been up in front of that many people to speak, so I naturally had the jitters. I must have peed a dozen times before I got up on the stage that day.

My mom had brought her camera for the event so she could document the entire thing. Unfortunately, she realized afterwards that she never loaded film into the camera, so there is no physical evidence of this event ever actually happening outside of my memory. Nevertheless, I made it through the speech. I learned years later

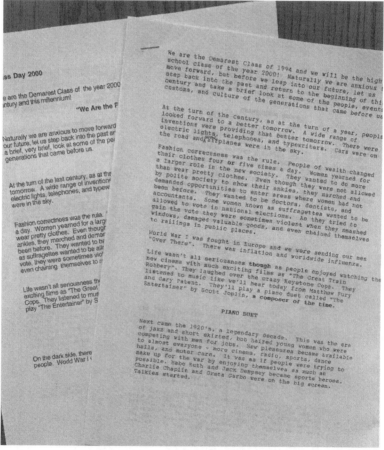

The original copies of the 1994 and 2000 speeches.

that my sixth-grade teacher used parts of it for the sixth-grade ceremony in the year 2000, which I referenced several times in my speech because I was in the high school senior class that year.

Luckily, our confidence for standing on stage and delivering words has improved since our time in school, but we meet adults all the time as we give speeches who say, "I would die if I had to stand up in front of others." And we wonder why we have students who have those same fears? Educators and parents, it is our responsibility to help our students find their voice (and our own) so that they can see that those fears can be conquered before they are adults.

In our experience, we have found that developing these skills at an early age is helpful. Younger students tend to be more carefree and uninhibited in front of peers. For many students, fear or embarrassment of speaking in front of others is a learned and reinforced behavior. Therefore, providing opportunities to develop and refine these skills in school, at all levels, is important.

STARTING SMALL: STANDING IN CLASS

When Adam was principal at Moore Elementary, he had a set of consistent classroom practices that were to be maintained in every classroom. One of those was standing to respond or speak. By standing to respond, students were forced to practice, in a low-risk setting, speaking in front of others. Todd also took this idea and ran with it while principal at Webb Elementary.

Do you ever have students who speak in class by putting their head down on the desk? It's hard to hear them, and they are reinforcing the practice of hiding when speaking. Another benefit of having students stand to speak is that the other students around them have a focal point to look at. When a student remains seated to respond in a crowded classroom, it is easy for classmates to ignore the speaker, especially because they can't see the student.

By learning to speak up in class, students are strengthening several leadership traits. Students will build poise and confidence as they overcome fears of others engaging themselves in what they have to say. They will also learn to monitor self-control in their speaking. This practice is helpful for children who have speech challenges such as stuttering, impediments, or lisps. Adam can attest to the power of practicing public speaking to overcome fears, as he suffered from both speech impediments and stuttering as a child. By having adults give him the opportunity to speak in front of others, he was able to gain confidence in his abilities and learn to slow down his speech enough to be clearly heard.

ADAM

When I first introduced to my staff this expectation of having students stand before responding, I saw my kindergarten teachers' eyes bug out. How would it be possible for five-year-olds to remember to stand when it is their turn to talk, they thought. What if they were too scared? Admittedly, I also was a little nervous for this to be a schoolwide practice. I had done this in my own classroom and in hundreds of model lessons taught across the country, but rarely had I done it with the youngest of students. But time and time again, remember that people rise only to the level of expectation you set.

Would you believe that of all of the school-wide rules and practices I put into place while principal, standing to respond became the most quickly adopted practice? If students ever forgot to stand, five classmates did not miss a beat in reminding them. After a couple of months, it became so natural that you would have thought they had been doing it for years.

With the practice well-ingrained, my fourth graders went on a field trip to Raleigh to visit the North Carolina House of Representatives. While there, they were sitting in the galley listening to the tour guide. When the guide asked the students a question, one of my students stood before responding. The tour guide said, "You don't need to stand," to which my student retorted, "Yes I do. It's what we do."

FROM STANDING TO SPEECHES

If you're a teacher, you can try a number of ways to ease students into becoming more comfortable speaking in front of others through your instructional practices. In addition to the simple strategy we laid out at the beginning of the chapter of having students stand to respond, strategies such as debate, Socratic seminars, literature circles, and book club groups are all methods that can be included across grade levels and curriculum.

Starting in a safe environment like the classroom is an easy way to build confidence for your students to be comfortable in front of others. As students get older, many more ways can be applied to continue growing this skill into leadership opportunities. Having students deliver speeches to run for things like student council, sports team captain, or club leadership positions allows students to use their words to convince others why they are the best person for the job. At school events or community gatherings, let students deliver an opening speech or recite a song or poem. In the long run, exercises such as these build poise and confidence in students' ability to share words and passions, which is an important form of expression and advocacy.

ADAM

Inspired by my own experience as a sixth grader, each year as a principal I told the fifth grade students that they would vote to select four classmates they wanted to hear make speeches at our school's promotion ceremony in June. To set the stage for the vote, I directed the students to nominate classmates who represented the school well. The nominees would be known for showing kindness to others and working hard; fellow classmates would be proud to listen to what the speakers had to say.

I was consistently impressed by how the fifth graders took this task seriously and made thoughtful nominations. The students always ended up with a fantastic group of peers who made heartfelt speeches in front of the audience. As I worked with groups over the years to prepare them for their speeches, the task came naturally to some. One student, Gabriel, had done a lot of acting outside of school and was simply a star onstage. He had learned his speech in one night and was at home in front of a large crowd. But several did not have confidence initially, and the training they received grew their speechmaking and leadership capacities. After all, team captains, club leaders, and even strong voices in the classroom all require the ability to speak up.

I also selected two kindergartners to speak at the fifth-grade promotion ceremony to close out the show, an idea I got from working at the Ron Clark Academy. At their eighth-grade graduation each year, two fifth graders would go up on stage at the end of the ceremony and wish the eighth graders the best of luck and thank them for their contributions to the school. I simply adapted that element to our elementary school and would find two eager kindergartners who could light up the stage and wanted to learn how to give a speech. They were always a hit!

Kindergartner Madeline addressing the audience
to close out the fifth-grade promotion ceremony.

If this idea of developing speakers is something you would like to adopt and you have students who require training, there are a number of important elements to teach, several of which can be brought back to SPECIAL The following are scripted guides for how to instruct on three elements when training your students:

- Posture. When delivering a speech, you need to maintain a posture on stage that people interpret as confident, even if you are nervous. Standing up straight with shoulders back and slight hand movements to emphasize points are small behaviors that can make a great difference in how people perceive you.

- Eye contact. When delivering a speech in front of a crowd, you want to connect with people for quick moments, and then move on. Do not forget the people in the back and on the sides. You want to engage the entire audience.
- Charm. When writing and practicing a speech, aim to elicit emotional responses. Laughter is a powerful reaction, so if you are able to get the audience to chuckle at a joke, you are likely engaging them.

ADAM

As with the recommendations for training greeters and ambassadors, feedback to your speakers needs to be immediate and specific. If the speech starts out rough, stop it early, correct it, and start over. I have had students practice just the first sentence of a speech twenty to thirty times before they get to move on. The goal is for them to develop *their* voice. If their voice sounded too robotic or too much like mine (since I typically modeled their speech), they started over. As I frequently shared with my students, "Practice makes permanent, so we're going to practice until we do something permanent that you feel comfortable doing in front of an audience."

I would usually begin the speech-writing process with students about four weeks from the speech's date of delivery. The students were responsible for writing their own speeches, but I worked with the students on editing and refining them. Students then practiced in my office for about two weeks during free moments in the day (e.g., before or after school and during lunch). About a week before the speech, I would take the students into the auditorium to practice onstage with the microphone.

A final recommendation for allowing students to make speeches is to not allow them to have the written speech in front of them when delivering it. It becomes a crutch and can alter the natural and personal sound of the speech. As I train students to make speeches without the paper, I encourage them to learn a speech, not to memorize it. By learning it, they are making it their own and using words and tones that sound natural to them. When students try to memorize a speech, forgetting a word or line often leads to their freezing up and struggling to recover.

SUPPORTING INTROVERTED STUDENTS

A question we get quite often when talking about public speaking is, What about our introverted students? Aren't we pushing them too far? True, public speaking will not be in every child's future, especially the introverts, but that doesn't mean we stop encouraging and challenging our students and helping grow every part of them, even if some aspects of their growth make them uncomfortable. For some students, developing their voice may mean building the courage to speak in front of just one other person.

ADAM

I had a soccer teammate growing up who was truly scared to speak to the coach. The child's fears likely translated to other areas of his life as well, but I witnessed it firsthand at soccer. The teammate would want to talk to the coach about getting more playing time or moving his position, and he just couldn't bring himself to do it. He grew so frustrated with his situation that he secluded himself from everyone. Looking back, I wish I had been a better leader and friend and helped him through it. Picturing my teammate in so much agony because of not being able to speak to the coach is a painful memory. Coaches, don't forget that you have an important role in facilitating opportunities to grow leaders as well. When you select a captain of the team, make sure the child understands that part of his or her duties is working with teammates to make sure all voices are heard.

At the same time, introversion might just be hiding a diamond in the rough; some students might not know they enjoy speaking in front of others but, once they do, can be crafted into excellent speakers. I taught such a student at Endhaven Elementary in Charlotte, North Carolina. The fifth grader, Elise, hadn't said more than two words in front of the class for the first month of school. She was as sweet as could be but never wanted to be in the limelight with any activity the class did.

At one point in the year, the class covered a poetry unit in which the students learned about shared voice from a book called *Joyful Noise: Poems for Two Voices* by Paul Fleischman. The lines in the poems alternated between person A reading, then person B reading, and sometimes persons A and B reading together. All the amusing poems are about insects and written from the insect's point of view.

Students were informed that they were to memorize their poem with their partner, dress up as their insect, and perform it in front of their parents at a poetry tea. Now, if I'm going to have an event where the parents come in, it's going to be good. We had practice after practice, and I am not soft when it comes to giving feedback, so we had some rough patches leading up to the tea.

Elise's partner had the first two lines, and they sounded decent. And then, with what seemed like a spotlight suddenly shining down in my room, Elise began her lines, "While I started life ..." It was the perfect first line for this young lady. This little girl, who remained quiet for so long in my room, simply came alive in reciting this poem. It wasn't perfect, but I saw something I had not known was there.

I began working with Elise during any little pocket of time we could find—recess, lining up for lunch, before school started—and we smoothed out some pieces of the poem to add a little bit of sarcasm to the voice here, a little bounce to the voice there. By the time the day of the poetry tea arrived, Elise was a rock star.

In Elise, leadership traits like creativity and enthusiasm emerged in the way she understood poetry and could turn it into something more than just words for her classmates. We could feel the passion she had for her performance grow each time she recited the poem. She also demonstrated courage and poise as she overcame her initial fear of speaking in front of others.

I was fortunate that I was able to hit upon Elise's interest in poetry and use that interest to bring her voice to the front. I know the reality is that I have probably missed several opportunities over the years with other students. You never quite know what can spark students' voice or pique their interest enough to move them to get up in front of others and shine. You just have to keep looking and creating those opportunities.

TODD

A different kind of support was needed in the case of a fifth-grade student I taught, Steven. He was terrified of public speaking. One on one, he was fantastic; put him in front of a crowd, and he would go blank. As the young man was debating on whether to run for student council, he met with me one day. He told me that he really believed he was the best person for the job but that he didn't think he'd end up running because the idea of giving a speech in front of the entire student body was almost too much to handle.

As I talked him through his own experiences of speaking (and his own insecurity and fears), I could see him loosen up. Young people think adults have it all together and that we don't struggle with the same things they do. The more vulnerable we can be with our students, the more they'll connect with us.

The student and I spent the next two weeks practicing his speech every day either at lunch, recess, or after school. We practiced in front of the first grade class and in front of the office staff. We even recorded it once just so we could see how it looked to others.

I'd love to say that on the day of the student council speeches he wasn't scared. But that would be a lie. He was terrified but determined. I remember him waiting to give his speech. Then he asked, "Mr. Nesloney, would you mind coming up, too, but standing off to the side of the stage where I can see you the entire time? That way, if it becomes too much I can look up and see you first and be reminded again of how badly I want this?" That day, he gave a rousing speech, full of emotion and heart. Anyone could tell this young man wanted the position! When he was finished, he received a loud round of applause. And, yes, he ended up winning.

CONCLUSION

Helping students to find their voice so they can use it to lead, whether formally or informally, is a valuable gift. Unfortunately, some of us adults still have not found our own voice, and we use that shortcoming as an excuse to reinforce students' discomfort or uneasiness with finding theirs. We say, "I turned out fine. They don't need to speak up." And we may have turned out fine, but that does not mean we should stunt the full potential of any child.

We live in a communicative world, and each voice is an important part of it. Find students you can help mold so that their voice—whether motivating, inspiring, or simply sharing—can be heard by others.

LEADERS' REFLECTION QUESTIONS:

1. What personal experiences as a child impacted your comfort level in using your voice as you got older? Do you still carry those sentiments with you today as you work with kids?
2. How do you currently help students find and use their voice on your campus or in your classroom?

Share on social media your favorite example of a student using their voice. Use the hashtag #WhenKidsLead.

7

CONFERENCES

A leader is a person who works hard every day to help others be better. They always take responsibility for what they say and do—even when they mess up.

—CATE, AGE 10

Educators talk about students a great deal. We talk about their latest assignments, their performance in sports, their attitude in class, their pasts and their futures. As educators we are invested in our students, and seeking to understand them is a top priority.

There are times in the academic schedule when the talk around students is formalized. We're talking about the oft-maligned parent-teacher conference. How many of you have been a part of this conversation?

Parent: "I'm concerned my son is coming home with Cs."

Teacher: "Yes, I've noticed too. His grades have been slipping."

Usually the next part of this conversation is about the student's not completing work, not studying for tests, sleeping in class, and so on.

All the while, the parent and teacher are stating observations and trying to put together pieces for why the child is not working up to his or her potential. Remedying these issues often comes with a plan made by the adults that the child is then expected to comply with. Rarely does it result in the desired turnaround.

ADAM

In an attempt to address the poor results of such a situation, I started inviting my middle school students into parent-teacher conferences to be a part of the conversation, because students often have more insight into their learning than either the teacher or parent does. This change brought the child's perspective into the mix. Sort of.

Parent: "I'm concerned my son is coming home with Cs."

Adam: "I've noticed he's been slipping in his grades, too. Devin, what have you noticed about your work recently?"

Devin: "I haven't been working as hard as I should be."

Adam: "Can you start working harder?"

Parent: "He's going to start working harder."

Devin: "Okay."

As I look back, I realize that the parent and I were still, at the end of the conference, making most of the observations and solutions for the child. The student had a chance to be heard and have his thoughts included, but it was just a courtesy for what ended up being an adult-centered conversation. The intent was for the student's voice to be heard, but the meetings were never properly structured for the child to lead the conversation. There had to be something better.

We educators have a sense that allowing students to take charge of situations is good for them and even good for us, but rarely do we stop and catalog the true benefits that stem from such a move. If we did, we might have to dramatically change our classroom practices to give greater voice to students. After all, if you discovered that giving students a say in their education was a win-win, could you reasonably argue that they shouldn't have a say?

And yet this is exactly what happens when students do get a say. In an authentic student-led conference experience, students are demonstrating honest reflection with their progress and ownership over their work. Cultivating such leadership traits through this practice would be invaluable; these skills can be carried throughout life and applied to many other personal and professional experiences they will face as adults. For teachers and parents, they are now witnesses to students showing responsibility through action. With students setting their own personal goals and the plans to achieve them, parents and teachers become facilitators and supporters of the process instead of authoritarians of student learning.

SHIFTING TO STUDENTS

ADAM

When I was the principal at Moore Elementary, my assistant principal, Tamatha Fullerwinder, had the idea to work alongside one of our second-grade teachers to create authentic student-led conferences. We had talked about trying this approach as a school for a while, particularly since we had implemented student-led data notebooks the year before. Students in kindergarten through fifth grade spent the year learning how to collect and track their own data. Each grade level did it a little differently, but students tracked data such as assessments, behavior, sight words, math facts, attendance, and meeting goals that they had set. They also learned to write reflection sheets so that when they did or did not meet a goal they could think about why that was and use that information to improve or continue that behavior next time. This practice increased ownership of work, taught goal setting, and motivated many students to work hard.

Giving students a year to learn how to work with data prepared us well to step up to the next level the following year. Mrs. Fullerwinder teamed up with second-grade teacher Brittany Protokowicz (Pro for short) to do student-led conferences with her class. The two worked with the second graders on continuing to collect artifacts and reflecting on their goals, the next step being that the young students had to learn how to summarize and verbalize their work to someone else.

Over the course of several months, students tracked their academics, behavior, attendance, and goals, and prepared a portfolio of work samples, data, and reflections. In the days and weeks leading up to the conference, students reviewed the data and came up with talking points they would share with their parent, family member, or guest on the day of the student-led conferences. The students derived these talking points by summarizing their data, a concept they were already familiar with from literacy instruction. Of course, the teacher modeled how to do this first, and then students received feedback from the teacher on the talking points they came up with. In the end, the students each had five to seven talking points to present. On the day of the conferences, the students then led a conversation with their parent and/or teacher. After finishing their conversation with a child, the adults rotated to another child. The children each experienced at least two or three adults listening to their student-led conference.

Ms. Pro decided to hold the conferences during the school day to ensure that every child would have a chance to share (since some would not have come if they were scheduled for the evening). We gave ample notice to the parents so that families were able to rearrange work schedules or ask a grandparent or family friend to join them. We also brought in several "backup" people (myself included) to join any student who did not have someone there. On the day of the conferences, all but one student had a family member or friend there, which was quite impressive! Plus, we had plenty of backup people in the room. Ms. Pro had also set up food and drinks, which were a nice touch for celebrating after the conferences were over.

The students were so proud to share their data notebooks. They carefully went through them, explaining the progress they had made throughout the year and noting certain areas for improvement. They interpreted their graphs, showing their progress on literacy assessments that were used by the state. Many talked about their behavior, which we tracked with Class Dojo, so they were able to show the number of points they were earning each day (we didn't take away points) and how the points related to work and academic trends.

The most beautiful aspect of this process was that every bit of information was coming from the student. Adults were not there to tell the students anything about their learning. We were there to listen and ask questions. The teacher even gave the adults prompt cards, which helped guide us in the questions we could ask. For example, "What subjects have you shown the most growth this year? How do you think you achieved that?"

I recall conferencing with a particular student for whom English was a second language. He did not speak much in school but had plenty to say during my time with him. After he completed his conference with me, I said to him, "That was excellent. Did you enjoy doing this?" He said with a big smile, "Yes, sir. It's easy talking about me."

In preparing the students to present, a number of the previously taught social skills came in handy. Students were able to use their SPECIAL training to remember to shake hands with the adults who listened to their presentation, introduce themselves to the adult if they did not know them, and listen to questions asked by the adults at the conclusion of the presentation, for example. To deliver their talking points, they used their eye contact and the confidence they had built from standing to talk in class. The teacher had taken the time to revisit all these training points in the weeks of practice leading up to the big day.

THE ADULTS IN THE ROOM

TODD

During my final two years as an elementary principal, we wanted to push my team to incorporate more student-led conferences. Our goal—even for our kindergarten students—was to help them track their data, reflect upon/analyze their data to set their goals, and generate their talking points. In the fall, my expectation, especially for second grade and above, was for the students to co-lead the conference with their teacher. That way, the conference was like a training session, but the students were still responsible for doing the talking. In the spring, my expectation was that students were leading their conferences on their own.

No two teachers carried out this process exactly the same. As a school, we went back and forth with whether to designate one specific method for collecting student data and include one specific set of talking points for these conversations. What we quickly learned was that every grade level (and oftentimes every teacher) wanted something a little bit different for their kids. Team by team, we sat together and crafted what the process would look like. As the school leader, I took part in every conversation so that the teachers clearly understood my expectations.

We knew that we wanted kids to be tracking their own data. That part wasn't necessarily hard to execute. The harder part came with training our students on how to have conversations about their data. We started with question stems that would help guide the students in second grade and above. For all grade levels, we also provided parents with a list of questions they could pose to their children to facilitate deeper reflections about their growth as students.

When we organized the actual conferences, we scheduled them to occur over a week's time, after school or during planning times. That way a teacher would be present to sit with each set of family members and help facilitate the conversation. If family members had deeper questions, the teacher would be readily available to answer them. Still, even though the teacher attended each conference, the purpose and intent was always to have the students talking to share their progress and what they had done to accomplish it.

The biggest takeaway from conducting student-led conferences on our campus was that the stakeholders—parents, students, and teachers—were a lot less likely to make excuses when everyone was around the same table listening and sharing. It never ceased to amaze me when a parent was shocked that we wanted their child at the meeting, too. Of course we do! We all play a role in student success.

Allowing the students to take ownership over their own learning gives them a platform from which to be proud of their work. Not only that, students are willing to be vulnerable and honest about the progress they have already made but also about the growth they still need to make. There is no adult telling them "This is what you're doing wrong" or "You need to start doing this." Each student has the chance to take their learning into their own hands, and there's something quite empowering about that.

CONCLUSION

If student-led conferences are something you envision in your classroom, here are a handful of helpful tips:

- Start by asking the students what types of data they believe is valuable to share. From there, ask them about ways to collect and track it.
- Before doing the real thing, model a student-led conference for the students. You play the role of the student, and let one of your students play the role of the parent or listener.
- Have students rehearse with partners many, many times!
- Limit conferences to about six to eight minutes. The idea is to identify important points and then support them with evidence. After the students share, have the adults ask questions for a couple of minutes.
- For older students, challenge them to find correlations between their artifacts. For example, a student may discover that a string of three absent days aligned with a test grade that was lower than the others for the semester.
- Remind students that there is no need to embellish or enhance the facts. This is their work, and the adults are present simply to listen and support them. At the same time,

students shouldn't be embarrassed to showcase their growth and accomplishments.

- Urge the students to be solutions-oriented. If their grades are not as high as they would like, have them consider ways to improve and the tools they would need to do so.

Remember, part of growing our kids into leaders is allowing them to take charge of their own path. They have to be taught how to use their voice to not only speak up for themselves but also share their journey and the work they do to get better. Again, this goes back to us as adults learning how to relinquish some control to truly let our kids lead.

LEADERS' REFLECTION QUESTIONS:

1. Why do you believe it is important to have students take ownership of their learning and progress? In what ways does a student-led conference promote student voice?

2. What kind of long-term planning is needed for you to successfully implement student-led conferences? What support or resources do you need?

Share on social media how your students have taken ownership of their learning through data notebooks, student-led conferences, or goal setting and self-reflection. Use the hashtag #WhenKidsLead.

8

CHOICES

A leader is someone who helps others. A leader is someone who works hard. A leader leads others. A leader makes others feel confident. A leader is someone who makes others feel better. A leader inspires others.

—CHARLOTTE, AGE 7

At its core, leadership is about making choices. Perhaps it's telling how infrequently students are allowed to make meaningful authentic choices. We're not talking about their choice of entrée at lunchtime or even a behavioral choice to act out or not in class but real choices about what their academic day is like and what they have to say about it.

Leaders have to learn to make choices that impact them and those around them. They have to be given the opportunity to explore and find the things they love. When we can show our students the power of choice in exploring different learning styles, we can help them develop who they are. Allowing kids to lead through showcasing their talents, skills, and interests beyond the traditional definition of "smart" builds confidence in our students and shows them that the world needs and desires people with diverse abilities.

Let's consider a couple of examples to get at this idea of the phenomenon of choice and leadership.

CHOICE BOARDS

It's the end of a math unit on area and perimeter, and you dig through your file folder to find the designated unit test. Your assessment is a mix of word problems, multiple choice, and a written response. In the end, you're hopeful that the students have learned the material well enough to pass the test so you can move on to the next unit.

We have done school this way for generations, and we understand that the practice won't disappear overnight. What if, however, you took a risk? What if you allowed the students to demonstrate their knowledge in different ways? What if they could prove to you that they understand area and perimeter without taking a traditional test?

Emerging assessment approaches, such as choice boards, are seeping into classrooms across the country as a means for teachers to empower students to use their passions, talents, and own perspectives to demonstrate mastery of the standards and curriculum.

Choice boards are presented in many ways. In a nutshell, students are given a multitude of choices for how they present their understanding of the material. It can resemble a tic-tac-toe board, though less than nine choices are certainly reasonable.

For a unit on area and perimeter, you might find that options such as constructing a 3-D LEGO model of a Minecraft creation or writing a song that helps learners understand area and perimeter would be appealing to students who are builders or singers. Students could take pictures of a building with a tablet or phone and then use the editing tools on the device to show measurements of the structure's dimensions. For students who prefer drawing, have them design a blueprint of the interior of a house. And for those who like writing, you can invite them to craft a story that integrates the concepts of solving for area and perimeter. Of course, if you have students who prefer traditional assessments, giving them that option is fine, too.

The opportunity for students to have a choice in how they demonstrate their knowledge is a powerful statement from you as the teacher. You are telling the students that you believe they are capable, and you want them to show you in their own way. And those students who learn early on that they are smart in different ways are going to understand that leadership traits can be derived from their intelligence.

For example, creativity is a highly valued leadership trait in many professional markets, and businesses are looking for thinkers who can express intelligence in various ways. They need leaders who can look at the same problem from different perspectives and collaborate to find a solution. If a company had solely a bunch of good test takers in a room, it may quickly realize that most real-world challenges aren't solved by filling in bubbles. Simply put, allowing our students to express freedom of thinking in their work and products sets them up to be more successful in their professional lives.

For help in making choice boards, consider Howard Gardner's theory of multiple intelligences. The traditional question asks, "Are you smart?" In light of the theory, the alternative question asks, "How are you smart?" Everyone has talents and abilities, but unfortunately, the definition of intelligence has been narrowed in our school test-taking culture. The multiple-intelligences approach encourages individuals to explore different modalities and discover ways in which they problem solve and create. By exploring this learning theory, you may be inspired to create choice boards that relate to the ways your students think best.

To generate an advanced version of the choice board, you can have students work in teams to create their own. From there, the class comes back together to share ideas and decide upon a final choice board for the entire class to use. Executing this approach requires even more trust in your students, but the ownership is tremendous!

ADAM

As a fifth-grade teacher, I allowed my students to take on the challenge of creating a choice board for the class at the completion of studying a series of books by Jerry Spinelli. I presented the students with a three-by-three grid and informed them that it would be their task to fill in the nine different options to choose from. The students met in small teams first to discuss ideas. Then, together we made a list on the board of every idea, combining similar ones. Next, we discussed having a broad range of ideas that would allow everyone to be successful. Finally, the students came to the board, each marking a check next to the three ideas that they were voting for. In the end, we had nine unique ideas ranging from writing a new chapter of the book to creating an interview with a character to filming a commercial.

While some of these ideas may sound like we're asking you to add another thing to your plate, we're not! Many times, the ideas we present are instead replacements for something you're already doing. As an educator, the more you engage your students and help them find the things they're passionate about, the easier your job becomes because you are creating a classroom culture of choice and ownership. Kids choose to lead only when they're impassioned by something. Let's help them find and grow those passions into something even bigger. Who knows? It could lead to a future vocation, a career—or even a movement!

MORNING CHOICE

ADAM

Since my district had a late start time, teachers had ample time to gather together before the students arrived. It was not uncommon for grade-level teams to meet and construct a full-scale breakfast buffet. The school was in a heavily commercial area, so these breakfast buffets were impressive with options—anything from a Krispy Kreme spread to Biscuitville biscuits to fresh pancakes made on-site, thanks to Mr. Hall and his awesome cooking skills. There was never a shortage of food at Moore Elementary!

In every classroom turned breakfast buffet, the teachers were chatting away. They chatted about television, talked about lesson plans, caught up on one another's personal lives, and shared gossip. Whatever the conversation, they were excited to be among each other and have the chance to be social.

Now, in many classrooms, when students start their day, what are they expected to do? Do they get to socialize with each other? Do they get to enjoy one another's company? In most cases, the answer is no. The typical routine is to enter silently, sit down at a desk, and start on a problem of the day, work sheet, or some other assignment. This practice has existed for eons, therefore it's reasonable to most educators to continue this expectation because it's how most of us grew up. And we survived.

But what if we challenged that system? What if we eliminated morning work and moved to morning choice, where students would have the opportunity to collaborate, create, innovate, play, and engage with one another?

ADAM

My quest for such a change started back in early 2017 when I was talking to Allison, one of my former college students. Allison was in her first year of teaching in Atlanta. She and I grabbed dinner one night to catch up, especially so I could hear how her first year was going. Allison is an eternal optimist. She sees the bright side of everything and is a go-with-the-flow type of person.

In fact, during Allison's student teaching, her cooperating teacher was playing outside with the kids during recess and tripped, tearing two knee ligaments. The teacher had to have immediate surgery, putting her out of school for the rest of the semester. This happened in October, so we were going to move Allison to another teacher's class. She decided though that she would stick with it and continue her student teaching in that class as their teacher. She's that type of person.

During our dinner, I asked Allison what one thing she would change to make her day easier. Without hesitation, she said her mornings. Her fifth graders had seat work to do each morning when they arrived. Some students would do it; others refused. Some finished early, some barely started. It was a constant headache for her to manage. And, frankly, the kids hated it.

I had had this idea about rethinking the start to the day in the back of my mind for a while, and this seemed like the perfect opportunity to try it out. I asked Allison if she would be willing to scrap her morning work and try an idea I called morning choice, in which the kids enter to a room of engaging board games, LEGO bricks, play dough, puzzles, art supplies, and more. She loved the idea and immediately implemented it upon returning from holiday break.

The shift changed the culture of her classroom almost immediately. Students were excited about getting to Allison's room. She no longer had to battle with them over doing work that wasn't looked at. Students had the chance to interact with one another, and their day was getting off to a much better start.

Much like choice boards, morning choice was allowing students to demonstrate smartness in different ways. Additionally, leadership skills were being developed in every corner. Creativity was nurtured as students designed creations out of LEGOs or Popsicle sticks. Fairness was fostered as students played board games without the constant monitoring of an adult. Kindness was promoted as students learned to invite newly arriving classmates over to play with them. Collaboration was exercised as students worked together to assemble challenging puzzles.

Success began to look different in Allison's class. The quiet kid who didn't have many friends was a fantastic chess player, and others started to notice his talent. The kid who was constantly doodling during math instruction was now making art pieces outside of art class. And, as with every classroom, great LEGO builders, puzzle solvers, and Monopoly players were revealed. These students may not have been the traditional academic standouts, but allowing them choice gave them a chance to shine and show their classmates their unique talents and skills.

Allison also made an explicit choice for leadership development in her room that was specifically geared towards fifth graders who wanted to work with younger students. During morning choice time, the students would go to a kindergarten classroom and assist the teacher with whatever needed to be done that morning. She told me that some of the most challenging students in her class made the best helpers in kindergarten.[2]

---

2 If the idea of morning choice interests you, please feel free to check out the blog post that Allison and Adam wrote at bit.ly/MorningChoice.

As principal, I decided that my school would embrace morning choice throughout all the grades. Each classroom implemented it during our staggered arrival time in the morning. This scheduling worked for us because it took place before instructional time. It also opened up time for us to work on our SPECIAL skills, as teachers would stand by the door and greet students as they entered the room. Ambassadors also conducted training during this time for greeters who needed practice. We were happy to find that, within the frame of morning choice, students were using select SPECIAL skills such as asking questions and listening to others while with their peers.

Adam's school implemented morning choice in each classroom.

As I talk about morning choice at conferences for educators, I explain that there's no one right way to do this—not even keeping it first thing in the morning! Some middle school and high school teachers have implemented the concept of morning choice into an advisory period or study skills activity, since many reported that their advisory periods were unplanned and unproductive. And teachers waiting on late afternoon buses to arrive have reported that they have adopted offering a choice period at the end of the day to help entertain the students. Think about your classroom's needs, and make it work for you!

CONCLUSION

Because of implementing morning choice, I have witnessed students excited to get to class, interact with each other, and learn from each other in nontraditional ways. I loved seeing teachers hop in to play board games or logic challenges. Even more entertaining was when the students beat the teachers!

I don't want to brag, but I am a pretty good Mancala player. Mancala is an ancient Chinese game that involves moving marbles, with the goal of taking into your possession more marbles than your opponent does. I had beaten several of my fifth graders already, and I was looking for new opponents. One day, I was challenged by Hailey.

Hailey was a sweet girl, quiet but fierce. She was known as an athlete and she destroyed most of the boys and girls in any sport. As we played our first Mancala match, I think I may have underestimated her a bit; she beat me! So, obviously, I needed a rematch after this defeat. I went harder this time, focusing more and aiming to destroy her. (Did I say I'm a bit competitive?) She beat me again.

I then became obsessed with beating Hailey at Mancala before she finished fifth grade. I ended the year 0–13. Hailey had already earned the class's respect for dominating in sports. With the Mancala wins, she gained a new respect by dominating their principal in an ancient Chinese marble game. Hailey exemplifies something that Hall of Fame basketball coach John Wooden calls competitive greatness. Leadership requires drive and determination. Hailey quietly showed those qualities in everything she did, and while other students may have been timid to go up against an

Adam and Hailey compete in a game of Mancala.

Hailey goes undefeated against Adam in her fifth-grade year.

adult, Hailey was not. I was proud to be on the receiving end of her competitive leadership.

I am proud that we were able to decrease our tardiness by over 30 percent as a school once morning choice was implemented. By tracking office referrals, we also observed a decrease in negative behavior during that time frame. Other educators across the country who have implemented morning choice report similar data trends.

Morning choice provides teachers a smoother start to the day. It creates a positive buzz around the school in the morning. But more important than the practical benefits of morning choice are the leadership qualities it promotes. Students gain confidence and demonstrate kindness, creativity, and fairness. They problem-solve issues and use their voice to make decisions. When kids lead using these skills, classrooms begin to look more student centered.

LEADERS' REFLECTION QUESTIONS:

1. What does the current morning routine in your classroom or school look like? Does it allow for students to lead?
2. What opportunities exist to shift toward allowing students to collaborate, create, and lead at some point in the day?

> Share on social media your morning-choice routine or other ways that students lead to start out their day. Use the hashtag #WhenKidsLead.

9

PASSION

A leader is someone who does risky things not knowing if it's going to work but does it anyway because it's the right thing to do.

—GRADY, AGE 10

Google has a practice in which employees on development teams are allowed to spend 20 percent of their time exploring and working on projects that interest them, provided that the side interests have the potential to advance the company. Google sees this as a way for people to explore their passions and ultimately increase productivity. From these projects have come products such as Gmail, Google Talk, and Google News.

Author and journalist Daniel Pink parallels this approach in his work on what motivates people. He explains that once work goes beyond rudimentary skills and requires cognitive or creative tasks, autonomy and self-direction lead to the greatest results.

He draws upon an Australian software company, Atlassian, which uses a similar approach to Google, in which they give their employees twenty-four hours once per quarter to work on anything they want with whoever they want, as long as they show the results to the company at the end of the period. The results have yielded both solutions to existing problems and ideas for new products.

The assumption in both of these examples is that people have an innate desire to explore what's interesting to them. When companies get out of employees' way and support them in going for it, products that may not have been discovered otherwise are often the result. These inventions were crafted when working outside the "office curriculum."

In school, students' opportunities to explore are traditionally confined within a set of curriculum options, such as when teachers instruct their students to explore a particular set of manipulatives or a specific book. Imagine a world where children have the chance to explore the topics that interest them inside of school but outside the curriculum.

As kids, we all had passions. We dreamed of becoming athletes, musicians, artists, firefighters, doctors, and so on. Some of us worked hard to capitalize on that passion, and it became a career. For others, the interest simmered away with age. Passion, though, is a driving force behind allowing students to develop as leaders. What if we could channel those passions into realizable projects—moving them off the back burner and letting them come to fruition within our classrooms and schools?

When we are passionate about something, working to learn more about it or becoming better at a related skill does not seem like work. When we enjoy something, we're doing it because of the love, not the salary. As parents, educators, mentors, and coaches, many opportunities inside and outside of school allow our children to explore their passions and show others their love for what they do.

And it's that love for and investment in a project that directly ties these activities to leadership. Leaders demonstrate creativity and innovation in their projects. The goals of the companies mentioned above in providing employees with open time was to create and innovate. These companies are developing leaders through project exploration. Essentially, teachers are doing the same in preparing students for authentic, real-world opportunities. Projects can also elicit leadership traits such as courage, kindness, and selflessness, particularly when the work of those projects benefits others in the community and beyond. Finally, students are building confidence in their abilities when taking on something they love, and so much of leadership rests upon belief in self.

Let's consider a couple of examples to examine further the phenomenon of developing student leadership through the pursuit of projects that students are passionate about.

PASSION PROJECT

ADAM

My friend Cindy was a phenomenal fifth grade teacher. Each year, she conducted a yearlong project that allowed each of the students to select a topic that they had a great passion for. It may have been a sport, hobby, or activity that they were interested in and wanted to learn more about. For some students, it was something they already had some knowledge of. For others, it was something they may not have been familiar with but wanted to learn more about. Throughout the year, the students spent time researching the history of their topic through watching videos, interviewing people, and other means to find out interesting facts, techniques, and new knowledge that would eventually become a piece of their culminating presentation.

On the presentation day of their passion projects, students would be spread across the cafeteria, each given a space to set up presentations, offer information, and show off materials to teach parents and guests about their passion. As I attended the showcase, I listened to students present about grilling, football equipment safety, dance styles, firefighting, and so much more.

One of the best stories from the passion projects came from two different pathways converging into one. Two young ladies started their individual journeys learning about two different topics: chemistry and space. They had spent the first two quarters of the school year becoming experts in their areas. In the third quarter, the two girls asked their teacher if they could combine their projects and make a spaceship out of lithium. They made a 3-D model of the spaceship, estimated the costs of a spaceship scaled to actual size, and examined the pros and cons of using the material. They put together a presentation to accompany the model and produced a passion project that combined knowledge with innovation and collaboration.

TODD

I also had a teacher friend, named Chris, who carried out a passion project with his sixth graders. Chris shared stories about the excitement within his science class but also the wonderment at what the students could come up with. My favorite story is of a student in his class who loved cars and wanted to learn how to build a motor from scratch.

At first, Chris sat with this student to dive into whether he was really capable of completing a task that seemed so monumental. After seeing the passion in his eyes, Chris couldn't say no. He was interested to see what this student would do.

Well, wouldn't you know that three months (and hundreds of YouTube videos) later, this young man had built a car motor completely from scratch in the classroom. It was incredible. And it was something that might never have happened in a more traditional educational setting.

It's inspiring to hear students not only be proud of the work they have done but become experts on their topic. Sometimes when teachers do these types of projects in school, we give students a few weeks to learn about their favorite animal or a famous person. And, yes, the students learn information and can talk about the more superficial facts. But can you imagine being a history major in college and having only three weeks to learn about your thesis topic? You need time and dedication to learn about your passion, and by giving the students a year to learn, they walk away with a greater depth of knowledge and appreciation for their topic.

That's why the best passion projects are slow-burning fires instead of conflagrations. The best of them are structured in a logical progression of identifying or discovering your passion, researching new information on the topic, and then presenting it to others. Each stage has its own opportunities for students to display a different facet of leadership. For instance, during the research stage, students can learn through more than just reading articles and watching videos; they can talk to experts and make face-to-face connections. In this case, students who have been trained on how to effectively converse with others will shine. SPECIAL skills such as asking questions and listening become essential competencies to successfully collect new information.[3]

---

3 If you are interested in doing passion projects in your classroom, we strongly encourage you to look into the Genius Hour movement and read *Pure Genius: Building a Culture of Collaboration and Taking 20% Time to the Next Level* by Don Wettrick.

As students get older, doing a project like this can evolve into action and the creation of real change. Students can begin by identifying a problem in their school or community and work individually or as a team to research the problem and present a solution. In their book *Teaching Toward Democracy*, Ayers, Kumashiro, Meiners, Quinn, and Stovall (2010)[4] share a story about a group of sixth-grade boys and their teacher. After a class discussion about immigrants' lives, the students were inspired to march through a large midwestern city along with one hundred thousand people fighting for immigrant rights. The only things the boys are armed with are two video cameras, posters, and a passion to tell a story. The boys would stop every so often and interview someone about the issues. Upon returning to school, they edited the clips down to a short documentary and created a community event to show the film. During the experience, they also learned about the history of prints and posters used in protests, discussed past and present social movements, explored the stereotyping of immigrants, and debated democratic access to and use of media. These young leaders demonstrated tremendous courage, creativity, and activism by taking on this pressing and personal topic and by creating community conversation around it.

CLUBS

The idea of pursuing one's passion and developing leadership qualities as a result is not limited to the academic realm. We see it all the time when a student develops a love of a sport and pursues that interest to become captain of their team. There's plenty written about leadership in sports, but there's another extracurricular realm that doesn't get the same level of attention yet is equally rich in opportunities for leadership.

---

4 Ayers, W., Kumashiro, K. K., Meiners, E. R., Quinn, T., & Stovall, D.
(2017). *Teaching toward democracy: educators as agents of change.*
New York; London: Routledge, Taylor et Francis Group.

Think back to high school. Did you ever feel out of place? Maybe it was difficult making friends. You wanted to fit in, and it wasn't by a lack of effort, but it just never felt right. But things changed when you met someone who was into the same things as you. This person introduced you to others who also had similar interests. Eventually, you decided to start a club based on these common interests. You found a teacher to be a sponsor, and you started up your club as a founding member. As membership grew, you realized that there were others around the school who also had that same interest; you just never knew it.

Clubs and organizations are a powerful way for students to develop leadership. They spawn from a passion you have inside and evolve into a means for you to share that interest and knowledge with others. Music, philanthropy, politics, sports, and art are just a few topics in which people find commonalities.

When thinking about the clubs at your school, how are you as a school or campus leader encouraging your students and colleagues to follow their own passions? Because when it comes to starting a club or organization, the adults have to be just as passionate (if not more so) than the students!

TODD

I remember when this concept really hit me hard. I knew that some of my team was getting burnt out by all the "have to do" and "data" conversations that were coming down from our upper administration. When I myself start feeling burnt out, that's when I begin bringing my own passions into my work to help it not feel so mundane. So I encouraged my team to do the same.

Little did I know that two teachers would come to meet with me and tell me about their passion for gardening. It was a stress reliever for them, but because they spent most of their time at school, they never got to do it. They wanted to start a gardening club! I immediately loved the idea (as I secretly had been wanting a garden on campus anyway) and encouraged them to run with it. Of course, being disciples of mine who I had taught about asking for forgiveness instead of permission, they had already reached out to the local lumber company and nursery about donating supplies and had assembled a group of students to help them along the way.

Less than two weeks later, they had a garden space designed and planted. Then one of the teachers found out about a three-day Junior Master Gardener training program that would teach them how to use gardening in every content area. Of course, I sent them to attend, and the information they came back with was fantastic. They were able to find ways to tie their own content areas into gardening, but even better, they were also able to train the remainder of the staff on ways that they could use the garden for academic benefits as well!

Less than six months after the creation of the garden, it was large enough and successful enough that we were able to open it up to the community to come and pick fresh fruits and vegetables, for free, anytime they wanted.

At the beginning of this project, the teachers took charge. They had ideas and goals for the school garden of their dreams. What the project quickly morphed into though was a collaborative experience between the adults and the students. I watched as the students began to develop new systems for watering the plants and research the most beneficial types of plants to include in the garden. Though this began as a passion project for the adults, the teachers quickly learned that their own personal excitement bled into the students, and the students in turn worked even harder to build something truly special that they took complete ownership of. Students all over campus were talking about their gardening club and asking how they could join.

The garden at Webb Elementary.

When I reflect on that experience, I'm reminded that leaders that do nothing but assign role after role take away some of the joy. When we leaders step back and find out what our team and students are passionate about and bring those passions into the school, we'll see people go above and beyond because they love what they're doing. And that passion will pour off onto the students, who will then take the leadership reins and run even further with the ideas than we ever imagined.

CONCLUSION

While it's perfectly understandable for people to pursue a passion they already have, never rule out the desire people have for learning new things.

ADAM

During my first year at the Ron Clark Academy, two of my colleagues and I started a LEGO robotics team after learning about it from competition organizers at Georgia Tech. Honestly, the three of us had little experience with robotics, but as a project it looked like fun, so we gave it a shot.

We found a group of kids who were interested in joining the team and we dove right in. If you're not familiar, the objective of LEGO robotics is to construct machines that will travel around a table-sized board and complete missions such as pushing or picking up objects, knocking down structures, and dropping items into places. The requirement is that your machine is built and programmed ahead of time.

The team was definitely into building the machines and strategizing on how to conquer the missions, but our project was stalled at that stage without someone to step up and program the machine to actually perform the actions.

Amy was a tiny girl, probably the smallest among her sixth grade peers. In class, she was quiet and sometimes overlooked for not being the vocal or animated one, but she was always polite and well-liked by her teachers. She just never sought out the spotlight. What I've learned, however, is that sometimes the spotlight seeks you.

She had previous experience with programming, and Amy's talents became the main driver of the team's success. Her ability to identify and troubleshoot problems quickly earned her respect among her teammates and allowed her to emerge as a true leader of the team. Other students would go to her first when there was a question and ask her advice on how to solve a problem with the machine.

We saw a true leader blossom out of a skill set and passion for what we were doing. As a team, we organized a structure of committees and tasks that needed to be cemented down (e.g., building, programming, and research), but the coaches allowed Amy to identify the students to put into leadership roles and work alongside to prepare the team for competition. The coaches met with Amy to discuss what her vision and ideas were for the team and then prepared her for executing them by having her write out a step-by-step plan of action for completing all the tasks. Over time, the adults were able to gradually release control and watch as Amy established a functioning infrastructure for the robotics team.

When the time came for Amy to consider high schools, she researched to find an option that would provide what she was looking for. She wanted to continue with her passion for robotics and programming and found a STEM academy in her district. After high school, it was only fitting that she chose to attend Georgia State University and major in computer engineering.

By no means would my colleagues and I take credit for setting Amy on the pathway to where she is now. But the fact that this team was able to provide her an outlet and opportunity to grow leadership traits such as confidence in her own abilities, selflessness in putting others in the spotlight, and productiveness for getting things done was likely an important piece in establishing a foundation for her future.

As adults, we have the chance to support our young leaders by sponsoring, coaching, or advising these clubs and organizations, since most schools require that an adult be associated with them. With your guidance, find students who are passionate about the topic and allow them to be in the driver's seat. Empower them to lead through their actions and words, and watch as they develop courage to take on new challenges, kindness to help others, and initiative to carve new paths!

Leadership can grow and flourish from the most unpredictable of places when fed by passion. Whether it's programming, building rockets or motors, or even digging in the dirt, adults have the ability to position students to blossom through projects that tap into interests outside of the curriculum.

LEADERS' REFLECTION QUESTIONS:

1. How did passion drive your interests as a kid? Did any of those passions grow or wither away as a result of the level of support from adults? Were you a part of a club or group that validated what you loved?

2. In what ways do you allow your students to use their passions, interests, and "smarts" to learn? What opportunities exist that you are not currently employing, and what resources are needed to make them happen?

Share on social media how your students are demonstrating knowledge and learning through their passions and strengths. Use the hashtag #WhenKidsLead.

PART
4

STUDENT COLLABORATION

Leaders are polite. They make sure things are fair and everyone is included.

—MILA, AGE 10

Elevation of the student voice is a solid standard for how you gauge kids leading in your classroom, team, or group. Our final section shares ways in which to advance leadership outcomes by working with others, becoming a supporter, and looking towards the future. Collaboration and leadership are relatively new phenomena in the professional world. Traditionally, leadership implied a top-down approach, where a bureaucratic structure labeled people by a title. The higher the title, the more leadership and decision-making were expected in that role.

Modern definitions, instead, focus on leadership at all levels of the workplace and require that people of any title perform in partnership. As a result, an individual's ability to not only lead but also know when to support becomes paramount. Previous discussions on listening skills emerge as one of the most vital traits that someone can bring to the table, as diverse and sometimes contradictory viewpoints are shared in one sitting. The courage to question and the honesty to disagree is crucial in today's world, and as children learn that collaboration is a means to derive the best outcome possible, early training on how to collaborate is key.

Student collaboration is examined from various angles throughout the following chapters. From connecting classes and students in various ways to leading by becoming a follower to developing one's career readiness through knowing how to seek help, we hope to provide you a starting point in your work. We do urge you to use these concepts as beginning steps only and to continue your own exploration and brainstorming of ideas on how to build student leadership through collaboration.

10

CONNECTING CLASSES

A leader is someone who stands out from others, someone who leads themselves or others to success. They help them succeed in life. They also help any way possible and strive to make theirs and others' lives right when they're not.

—DIONYELL, AGE 14

Living and working within a silo limits one's ability to grow and learn. The ability of stepping outside one's circle is incredibly powerful, as it uncovers new ideas, fresh perspectives, and greater networking opportunities. Leadership naturally springs from new interactions, as we are suddenly confronted with choices to share or listen to original information, create novel relationships, and collaborate on tasks. We can choose to stand at the forefront or wait to the side; speak up first or listen to gather information; promote innovation or follow guidelines. Endless possibilities emerge as new combinations of thinkers come together for the first time.

Connecting students face-to-face and through technology adds value to each participating member's learning and leadership growth. Students are building awareness for an outside perspective and experience, particularly if the partnership spans cultural, age, or geographic lines. They are learning appreciation for others' work, especially when the collaboration leads to a collective product. And they are inspiring positive character displays from each other, such as kindness and empathy, as they learn about each other and build relationships. Please note that these skill sets (as discussed in chapter 2) are important for children to learn before entering a collaborative setting. Without the establishment of these prerequisites, students are left to suffer potential harmful experiences in working with others.

We would be remiss not to acknowledge that the natural block to these collaborations described ahead are not with the students but with adults. The risk of making connections outside of your classroom, school, or district is perilous in some people's minds. Many safe and productive ways to connect abound, and frankly, it has never been easier to reach out and make those bonds, as we live in a digitally connected world. As for the students, many, if not all, will rejoice at the chance of having a new person to call friend.

CROSS-GRADE-LEVEL COLLABORATIONS

TODD

I have witnessed the power of cross-grade-level collaborations. I remember as a classroom teacher always searching out ways for my students to learn and interact with kids outside our classroom yet still on our campus. Oftentimes when we think of cross-grade-level collaborations, we jump straight to academic improvements. But we can collaborate just for the sake of growing better kids.

One of my favorite collaborations I did was with our Preschool Program for Children with Disabilities (PPCD) classroom. When I taught fifth grade, I wanted to grow empathy in my students for all the kids they would come in contact with. Lucky for me, right next door to my classroom was our PPCD classroom. While brainstorming ways to collaborate with other classes, I reached out to the PPCD teacher to get her take. She helped walk me through many of the daily challenges her students face and felt that some of my students might not be ready to work with kids with such high needs. But try we would!

I brought my entire class into the PPCD room the next day to help them do a quick art activity. Immediately, I could see the natural caretaker in many of my students when they stepped right up. Yes, some of my students were standoffish for a while, but eventually they all warmed up to the simple belief that kids are kids.

As the year progressed, I found that more and more students were asking for ways that they could go into and help our PPCD classroom. I started creating time within our schedule for them to be able to pour into others. Their volunteering never took from instruction time, but sometimes students finished their work early, leaving them with some free time when I could send them in to be an extra set of hands. It was such a joy to watch some of my students come alive and their eyes sparkle as they worked in the PPCD room with students who they felt needed them more than they had ever felt needed before.

When it comes to collaborations between grade levels, you really are only limited by your own creativity. The following are a few of the favorite collaborations we've been a part of ourselves or witnessed others doing.

- Book buddies – Watching students in different grade levels bond over books is one of our personal favorites, whether they are reading a book together, discussing books, or even comparing how to determine a main idea or practicing inference skills. Leaders are building patience and kindness with these activities, and under certain structures might also be building speaking and listening skills during discussion. Seeing an eighth grader down on the floor reading a book and talking through the characters with a kindergartner warms even the coldest heart.
- Science lab partners – If you study science standards, you'll find most of the standards either build upon each other or spiral as students matriculate through the grades. Imagine partnering your students up with a different grade level and having them learn (or refresh their learning) around the same core standard.

ADAM

When I taught fifth grade, I partnered up with a second-grade teacher during our ecosystems unit to have our students do an activity together on habitats and the food chain. While the vocabulary was richer for my fifth graders, the core standard overlapped, and it made for a great collaboration and leadership opportunity for my students. The fifth graders discovered their role as facilitator and guide for the younger students instead of wanting to simply do everything themselves. In this situation, the fifth graders' part shifted to that of teacher.

- Reteach –We all know that teachers can say something one hundred times to students, but sometimes it takes someone their own age to say it for it to stick.

TODD

I loved being able to have my students help younger students with difficult concepts. Fractions seemed to be one of those topics in our math class. As we learned about fractions in fifth grade, there were still fundamentals that my students struggled with. So what did we do? After I taught my fraction unit and felt my students had a firm grasp, I partnered with the teacher of a third-grade class. My students went into her classroom to teach their third-grade partner about fractions, but at the younger level. The fifth graders showcased courage in this exercise, as many of them were still not completely confident in their own ability. However, when the bar is raised and leadership opportunity sits in front of you, students will find a way to rise to the occasion.

- The arts – Dance, theater, music, and literary and visual arts are all means for people to explore ideas and communicate with each other. Exposing students to the arts at a young age can lead to interests in areas that they had not previously considered.

ADAM

As a teacher, I reached out to a local high school theater class to see if they would be willing to partner with our class on a performance that I was producing with my students. We had read several stories based on classics, such as *Peter Pan, Rumpelstiltskin,* and *Robin Hood,* from a series called Steck-Vaughn Point of View Stories. The students split into two teams and produced a short reenactment based on the point-of-view tale they had read. Not only were the high school students overjoyed to come down to the elementary school and help the younger students write scripts, rehearse, make scenery, and learn to act, but the high schoolers developed empathy for students who struggled with the process and patience as they allowed the younger students to develop their thoughts.

- School news – Many schools show a live or pre-taped news-cast each morning to share information, celebrations, and fun facts. While this duty is typically reserved for the oldest kids in the school, consider ways in which all students can participate, even if the older students still manage the show but learn to facilitate, instruct, and direct the younger students.

ADAM

At Vienna Elementary, the first school I worked at, my fifth graders ran the morning news by writing, directing, and filming it each morning. However, it was a long-standing tradition that after the first couple of months of school, each grade level would rotate through the anchor job as the fifth graders produced the show. By the end of the year, even kindergartners were reading the morning news. Additionally, toward the end of the year, the fifth graders would train a group of fourth graders (much like Todd's social media interns), so that they would be prepared to take the reins the following year.

TECHNOLOGY AND COLLABORATION

We understand that finding time to collaborate is challenging, and not simply because of other demands on one's time. Schedules might not line up, or classes might find themselves on different tracks that limit their ability to physically connect for collaboration. Thankfully, today's technology can be used to overcome these limitations. Let us share with you two examples of technology that we've applied to our work with great effect. Do understand that there are many different ways you could use different technological tools to achieve similar ends.

The first tool we want to focus on is called Flipgrid. We love Flipgrid for so many reasons. Not only is it free for all educators but also it is incredibly easy to use, for both teachers and students. Essentially, Flipgrid allows you to create a space for students to easily record and upload video responses to a task at hand. You control the privacy settings such that you can allow only the teacher to see their video responses, or you can open it up to allow all the other students in the class to see and be able to comment on the responses of their peers.

Flipgrid is a great tool to use to ensure that students are completing an assigned task. Imagine setting up a station with a bowl containing slips of paper with questions stems or scenarios written on them. When students get to that station, they pick out a piece of paper and record their response to the question or scenario in Flipgrid. When the next group rotates through, they must first watch a response that has already been recorded and provide constructive feedback. They then record their own response to a chosen question or scenario.

Or what about reading with others? We talked about book buddies previously. But sometimes maybe you're not able to partner up your classroom with another classroom. Maybe the book buddies you want to match up with are on a different campus in the same district. So how do you make that work?

We love seeing tools like Flipgrid solve this dilemma. Imagine creating a Flipgrid where each of your students reads and discusses a book that has deep meaning to them. Maybe it showcases their culture, personal interests, or home state or country. You can then share your grid with the teacher of the class you are collaborating with.

That teacher then allows their students to watch and respond to their book buddy's video. The beauty is that the interaction occurs on any schedule that works for the teacher. Even better, students will build understanding and compassion for another human being, which is a vital leadership trait for any student to learn.

Another excellent technology tool is videoconferencing. Whether you're using platforms such as Google Hangouts, Skype, Zoom, or something else, the particular tool isn't what makes this technology one of our favorites. It's the idea that you can collaborate with anyone, anywhere in the world, for free, through video!

The power of video cannot be overstated. Students love the ability to connect and interact. Although Flipgrid is a great tool for collecting video snippets, sometimes you want or need to hear or interact with someone live, not through a recording. Videoconferencing software allows you to invite in authors, other classrooms around the world, athletes, family in other states, and so much more, to collaborate in a myriad of ways.

Really, the only thing standing in your way is your own imagination!

CONCLUSION

Collaborations do not need to be contained between strictly traditional classrooms and teachers. Remember, collaborations between students is a broad notion and can include many other innovative ideas. One idea is to have your classroom write a school newspaper and interview or cover a school or local sports team or club. The students can learn how to conduct interviews, collect statistics and quotes, and write a newspaper story. Teach students that reporters use journalistic integrity and show leadership by reporting on facts.

Another idea is to connect students through a common mission, such as volunteering or philanthropy. While there are certainly traditional content standards that can be tied to a volunteering project, the goal of this endeavor is to have students be activists in their community and beyond. By connecting with others to partake, you are spreading the message that service requires everyone. Some examples of service projects might be connecting with other schools to have a lake cleanup day, participating in a charitable race, or creating a chorus to sing at a retirement home. For those classrooms connecting outside of community lines, you can collaboratively create letters to soldiers (using word-processing software such as Google Docs) or create a joint online GoFundMe campaign for a favorite charity, for which the collective group of students work together to create promotional material and advertising. By empowering students to be selfless and kind, we are building a future society where giving back becomes the stuff of everyday expectations, not viral videos.

There is a wealth of knowledge and leadership to tap into at every school. As you walk up and down your hallways, keep a keen eye out and your mind open for opportunities that might exist for partnering with a colleague or grade level to enrich your curriculum, enhance a skill set, or build leadership within your students. Look outside your hallways as well to consider other groups within the school community but also those beyond it. We live in a rich and diverse world, and connecting your students to others is a powerful way to grow young leaders. Through these practices, students are learning to work with others—sometimes older, sometimes younger—and understanding how to adapt and scaffold language and content, which is an invaluable skill in the professional world, where we need to convey information of all kinds.

LEADERS' REFLECTION QUESTIONS:

1. Is collaboration currently encouraged in your school? If so, how are you currently collaborating with others? If not, is there an opportunity to break the script and start this practice or reach out beyond your school walls and connect with people outside your campus?
2. How can a collaborative activity, lesson, or game increase learning and promote leadership for your students?

Share on social media how your students collaborate with other students and how it promotes their leadership skills. Use the hashtag #WhenKidsLead.

11

LEADING
BY FOLLOWING

A leader is somebody who sets an example that is worth following and inspires positive change in others. True leaders care about the people around them and want to see others succeed. They will have a passion for a cause bigger than themselves and focus on the wellbeing of the whole rather than the individual.

—LEXI, AGE 18

Throughout this book we have shared examples of how adults can inspire, empower, and grow young leaders by putting children in roles or situations that will enhance their confidence, develop their skills, and equip them with the tools to grow as leaders.

Sometimes, however, the greatest leadership one can show is to follow others. Not everyone can be at the helm all the time, nor should they be. There comes a time and place where even the strongest, most effective leader must step back and become a follower. By helping others realize that following is a form of leadership, you are actually empowering them to step up.

This is an important point that too frequently gets swept under the rug when talking about leadership. Good leaders know when to project their leadership, but also when to check it for the best outcome to emerge. To that end, an important part of teaching students about leadership is to get them to recognize that the point of leadership is not simply to lead but to lead to a desired outcome. And sometimes reaching that desired outcome requires a leader to become a follower.

THE FIRST FOLLOWER

There is an excellent video that you can find on YouTube called "First Follower." It's a grainy video of a shirtless guy dancing freely on the lawn at an outdoor concert. At first, the dancer appears weird because he's the only one dancing. We've all seen this before at a concert or festival where there's that one dude just dancing like he ain't got a care in the world. That's this guy.

After half a minute, someone from the crowd joins him. The first dancer no longer seems weird because someone has joined him. This attracts another person to join, and another, and over the course of just three minutes, the vast majority of this crowd has joined the dancing.

The important piece of this video is that it was the first follower who validated the efforts of the shirtless dancing guy and showed that his idea of crazy dancing was not so crazy after all. In fact, the first follower was actually being a leader (for the rest of the crowd) by following (the dancing guy). (It sounds strange even typing it, but think about it.)

When we hear the word *follower*, it is frequently accompanied by something negative and along the lines of "Don't be a follower" or "If he jumped off a bridge, would you do it, too?" However, being a follower in the right situation is actually a good thing. It takes a special person to know when and how to properly follow someone so that you are investing in that other person, usually publicly for others to observe and follow suit.

By investing in someone else, you are explicitly or implicitly saying that you believe in him or her. It's not to say that the person you are investing in has all the answers, but you are willing to join that person on the ride in pursuit of their goal. You are showing selflessness, as long as you do not boast of your actions. In some cases, your justice-oriented mindset is on display when you support a traditionally marginalized voice.

Even as adults, we do not always know when to follow. You're at a park and the trash can is full, so someone puts their trash on top of the can. Others see this act and do the same. Not a good follower. Someone begins shouting racist remarks at a person, and others join in. Not a good follower. Someone bullies a classmate, and others side with the bully. Not a good follower. You get the point.

We are constantly watching people around us to try to make sense of what is socially acceptable in a given situation. How else do you think kids learn (rightly or wrongly) table manners, bathroom etiquette, and school behavior? For better or for worse, we often trust what we see as the acceptable thing to do, even when it's not.

What we have outlined thus far are two parallel, but distinct, guiding principles. The first is teaching students how to choose the right course of action when the stakes are low, such as littering, holding the door open, and saying thank you. These are issues of character and habit, and it's worth identifying them as such and distinguishing them from what comes next, which is being an ally and preventing harm from coming to others when the stakes are higher. Issues of acts of bullying, racism, and violence are examples that would qualify here. Both of these types of activities are important, and both require adults to be explicit in the identification and teachings of when and where following is an appropriate route.

HOW TO LEARN TO FOLLOW

It becomes important, then, to teach children how to determine when to follow and when to ignore or speak up against a negative act. Lessons on culture, acceptance, diversity, tolerance, and history are imperative so that students can discuss and deliberate situations that deem following as a positive decision.

In the appendix we share titles of texts that will help students become more aware and knowledgeable about the diverse range of people they may meet in life. Equally important, though, is giving our students experiences that will test their ability to make sound decisions when presented with tough choices and peer pressure.

Role-playing is a powerful activity in which students can insert themselves into scenarios where they have to decide whether to follow someone. In the 1980s and 1990s, you may recall the anti-smoking and anti-drug television commercials that were constantly shown. Remember "This is your brain. This is your brain on drugs"? If you did drugs, your brain would crack open onto a skillet and turn into a fried egg, or at least that's the message we interpreted.

ADAM

I recall having D.A.R.E. classes in elementary school. If you are not familiar, D.A.R.E. was a law enforcement initiative started in the 1980s where officers would come into classrooms and speak to students about drug prevention, membership in gangs, and violent behavior. We would role-play situations and have to practice saying no to someone trying to offer us drugs. I brushed it off at that young age since it didn't seem like anything I would ever face. Little did I know that just a year or two later I would be faced with middle school kids offering me cigarettes in the school parking lot as we rollerbladed through the stairwells. (I said no by the way.)

As important as it is for students to practice saying no and reacting appropriately in negative situations, it is just as valuable to model examples of positive behaviors. Here are a few scenarios you can model with your children or students to show them when it is good to be a follower.

- An elderly person has fallen down, and you see someone trying to help her up.
- A classmate has started clapping for someone who has done something well in class.
- Your brother or sister is starting a campaign to collect clothing to help those in need.
- Someone is holding a door for people to exit, but there is a second door that could be opened and held.
- One of your classmates wears a hijab, and during recess, it falls off as she is dribbling the soccer ball. Someone stops playing for a moment so she can put it back on.

Again, by being a follower in any of these situations, the second person is showing awareness of and validation for the first person's effort, kindness, and integrity. His or her willingness to follow is ultimately a form of leadership.

Being a follower is hard for some students. They are naturally drawn to the spotlight and enjoy being the one "in charge." These are the most important kids to do these activities with. You may also need to be more explicit with these types of students, because subtle or implicit suggestions may not be understood by them. If you have a student like this, don't be afraid to say, "This is Jordan's moment. You have had your chance and now you need to support him."

ADAM

One year, I had a student named Hannah who was what many would consider to be a mother hen to her classmates. She loved taking care of everyone, which was admirable, but it got to the point where she was not letting her classmates do anything for themselves. Lower-performing or lazy students would just ask Hannah to do it for them, and she would happily oblige. I didn't want to destroy her giving spirit, so I tried to gently encourage Hannah to let her classmates do the things they needed to be doing for themselves, like answering their own questions, cleaning up their own messes, and packing up their own book bags.

The adjustment worked for a few days, but then the habit came back. I spoke to her parents about it, and they supported my taking a more direct approach. I let Hannah know that while I appreciated her loving and supportive heart, she was enabling her classmates. I did not want to completely eliminate her leadership, so I ended up making her "helping hand" cards. I gave her three cards to start the day, and each time she did something for someone, she had to give me one. If she showed to be an effective follower for someone else by encouraging without doing for them, she could earn one back.

Over time, Hannah learned that following others was just as pleasing as helping them. I eventually weaned her off using the cards, and she figured out how to find a balance between leading by doing for others and leading by following.

FOLLOWING ACTIVITIES

Role-playing and coaching are both critically important avenues for students to begin exploring how to follow. But there are a host of other activities that students can perform that teach this vitally important message about leading and following.

TODD

One of my favorite activities to do with students was flipping the tarp. The idea is simple. Lay out a tarp flat on the ground, have all the students stand on it, then, as a group, they try to flip the tarp completely over without anyone falling or stepping off the tarp.

It sounds easy enough—until you realize how difficult it can be. One of the biggest reasons I had my students do this activity is that it teaches the importance of communication. It also conveys the idea that those who are natural go-getters and loud leaders aren't always the best people to lead in this situation.

When students inevitably fail the first few times, I stop them and ask, "Who in your group are you not seeking ideas from? Who is remaining quiet?" When I ask them to reflect, they quickly realize that the person who wasn't saying much had instead been watching what was happening very closely. When given the chance to lead and the opportunity to use their voice, the quiet observers had a solution! Usually it was the right one. A great discussion follows this activity, and it's not uncommon for initial leaders to realize that when they became followers and allowed others to lead, the task got completed.

Anytime our class became a room full of arguments over everyone trying to lead, we would quickly pull out the tarp and remind ourselves that sometimes we need to take a step back, listen, and follow.

Another great activity is to put students into pairs and have them decide which of the two will be blindfolded. The blindfolded student is then guided through a series of tasks by their seeing partner. This activity is great to have all the students in your class do at the same time. That way you can also include a conversation about distractions and how those play a role in someone trying to lead. Through this, students are learning how using specific, clear language and focused, keen listening are both critical skills that leaders and followers must possess to be successful together.

One final activity that helps show the power of being a leader and a follower is the human knot. In this activity, have a group of students form a circle. They then reach across and take the hand of someone across the circle. It is important at this stage to stress to students that they need to have their left hand grab the left hand of someone else, and the same with their right hands. If they do not heed this advice, the activity will still work, but it will be way more complicated! Students then work together to unknot their arms and form a complete circle again, without ever letting go of any hands. Again, like with the tarp and blindfold activities, students learn to manage their own desires to be the boss and to accept leading by following.

CONCLUSION

At times, excelling as a follower can be as complex as excelling as a leader. Students should be constantly looking at ways to support another person but also respectfully integrating their own perspective and narrative, only not at the detriment of the task at hand. To effectively accomplish this, kids need to continue developing and using valuable skills such as asking questions and listening. Asking questions of the leader, such as about his or her goals, mission, and vision, can help the followers formulate a better idea of where the leader is heading and how to best provide support.

When kids become effective followers, they may exhibit similar leadership traits as when they lead, but how these traits present will differ. A follower may show courage, but this courage will contrast with the courage exhibited by the leader. The follower's courage may take the form of the willingness to step back and watch others first, while the leader's courage may take the form of stepping forward to take on something unfamiliar.

Be on the lookout for those kids who are great followers. Compliment them. Recognize them. Thank them. An effective follower is one of the most important and valued positions in leadership. No famous leader has ever achieved anything without a loyal follower. And all those great leaders would likely be quick to mention that their best follower was an equally great leader. What a great skill to teach all of our kids.

LEADERS' REFLECTION QUESTIONS:

1. Do you have any students who consistently show leadership by following? What do they do that helps empower others?
2. How do you teach kids to know when to lead and when to follow? Why is that an important skill for life?

Share on social media your tips or ideas on how to teach students leadership through following. Use the hashtag #WhenKidsLead.

12

CAREER DEVELOPMENT

"A leader is not afraid to do the right thing because they know it's for the greater good."

—BRODY, AGE 12

People who conduct job interviews will likely say that there is a generally expected set of behaviors and courtesies that candidates should demonstrate during an interview. As talent pools for jobs become more competitive and as the expectation to come career-ready increases, explicit personal and career training is essential for our youth before they step into that first interview. This is not just practical advice; the ability to present yourself and your accomplishments is a key asset for any good leader.

ADAM

When I was a visiting clinical professor at Wake Forest University, I discovered that one of the most sought after services by students was the Office of Personal and Career Development. There, students were able to talk to professional counselors about career opportunities, networking, mock interviews, and résumés.

Students lucky enough to attend a college or university that offers such services have access to top-notch connections, leads, and direction on how to enter the professional world. Further, some children are fortunate to grow up in a home or community where they are observing adults model behavior on how to network and small talk. Others find advantages in being well traveled or knowing how to quickly acclimate to new surroundings. These skills invariably mold a person's ability to feel comfortable and thrive in high-stakes situations such as interviews. And invariably those same skill sets are the skills that leaders possess in spades.

As educators, we have no control over our students' circumstances before they reach us. And students certainly can't control where they're born. But adults have the ability to control how each child is expected to learn. When caring adults expect more, children give more. In schools, sports, clubs, and places of worship, adults have the opportunity to build and facilitate the acquisition of knowledge. As the saying goes, "Knowledge is power." We want our children to feel powerful and confident in their abilities. And while access to resources will vary, building confidence, courage, creativity, and integrity in a child transcends race, economics, sexual orientation, gender identity, and ability.

Building these leadership traits, however, should not begin at age eighteen. Starting at a young age, we need to educate *all* children about how differences shape who we are, because unfortunately, differences can alienate. Differences can scare people. Differences can sever relationships. Differences can inhibit individuals from obtaining jobs or opportunities.

The remedy is for us to come to an appreciation of differences through conversations about race, gender, ethnicity, sexual preference, and social class beginning at an early age. Through this work, we will better shape understanding and collaboration among diverse individuals. And ultimately, it is the commonalities in human experiences—happiness, sorrow, fear, loss—that bring us closer together. When we allow children to participate in open dialogue about what makes them who they are, we are telling them, regardless of their circumstances, "You belong." Leaders not only thrive under those conditions, but they are key to making them manifest.

Poised confidence in one's abilities and makeup naturally leads to development in other areas. Once children feel like they belong in a space, they are ready to gather the tools to remain there. The call for inclusive programs where students can receive training and tips on personal and career development is crucial. Without them, students will not have the opportunities to collaborate with others in the professional realm, which limits future leadership opportunities. It is up to the adults in children's lives to provide intentional lessons and opportunities surrounding these topics.

We encourage that programs and courses covering life skills, financial management, and citizenship (in the sense of being a contributing member of society) be present at all levels of schooling. Based on our experiences, we share a starting list of important competencies that can and should be taught to all children.

RÉSUMÉ BUILDING

The résumé. A snapshot of you. This document is typically a page or two covering the education, job experiences, special skills or talents, and other information that a job candidate would want a potential employer to know in order to get in the door. The résumé is simply that: a ticket in.

The art and science of putting together a résumé is a tricky one, particularly because there are so many possible ways to construct this important document. Some professional fields prefer using certain formats or including certain information. Even certain jobs may require particular highlighted facets of information.

TODD

Recently I spoke in front of a group of future teachers at my alma mater, Texas A&M University. I still keep in contact with one of my college professors, Dr. Robin Rackley, who asked me to present. I have a special bond with Dr. Rackley. Why? Because of an embarrassing thing with my résumé—a story, still to this day, she shares with each of her college classes!

You see, I was in Dr. Rackley's senior methods class. I was preparing to head out on my first interviews in hopes of securing a teaching job. I was over the moon to already have several interviews lined up, and so I asked my professor for advice. The first thing she asked was for my résumé. I proudly showed her what I had googled and typed up. She started laughing immediately and then asked me if anyone had ever taught me how to write a résumé. Well, of course, no one had. I had just googled what good résumés look like!

Little did I know that you should have sections and details in a certain order using the same font and a bulleted format—and you don't have to list a thousand things. Right then and there, she sat down with me and helped me rewrite my entire résumé. And guess what? I got that job! And today in Dr. Rackley's class, she always dedicates a section in her course to writing a résumé. (You're welcome, future Texas A&M graduates!)

As principals, we saw hundreds of résumés come across our desks. All employers will have their own list of preferences they look for in a candidate's résumé, but there are definitely some general practices that most employers agree that teachers need to convey to their students.

Format properly: Make sure the margins are even, spacing is consistent, and font size and style is appropriate.

Edit: The spell check tool is your friend. Use it. Also, have a second set of eyes look over a résumé because a spell checker will not catch certain things (like homophones).

Avoid verbal diarrhea: Explain your previous jobs with brevity in mind. You don't need to chronicle your daily schedule, especially if it's a self-explanatory position. For example, teachers don't need to include that they wrote lesson plans and taught students. Those duties just come with the territory.

Interestingly enough, there have also been new trends emerging on résumés because of the many templates now available.[5] Trends we have noticed are people placing their photo in the résumé, adding their social-media handles, and providing their reference information up front. Following these trends or not, it is important that the résumé reflect the individual and the goal. With the abundance of free online resources, creating a résumé is not as scary as it used to be. Learning how to do so should be a staple in every child's education.

ADAM

As a fifth grade teacher, I had my students create a résumé to apply for classroom jobs. Obviously, the list of experiences and accomplishments is not long at age ten, but the practice was what mattered. This was before digitally generated resumes, so I taught my students the techniques of lining up margins, thinking about spacing, and using appropriate font size. (Why do kids always want to use font size 36 when they type?!)

---

5 On Microsoft Word and websites like MyPerfectResume.com, Indeed.com, and ResumeGenius.com.

If your school offers technology classes or computer lab time, or you teach writing, consider introducing the résumé-writing process into the instruction. Parents, this is a great activity to do with your own children at home as well. You know your child's strengths and activities best, so you can help as they practice getting them down on paper.

MOCK INTERVIEWS

ADAM

During the spring semester each year while teaching at Wake Forest, I taught an educational-leadership course to elementary education majors. As one of the culminating activities, I would invite local principals to come in for a round of mock interviews with my students, who were about to enter the teaching profession. Each student had five minutes to interview with between eight and ten principals so they would experience different styles of questioning.

To prepare, we talked about the dos and don'ts of interviews specific to education. Here are a handful of the things that we typically discussed, which you will notice are closely tied to the SPECIAL training and the various leadership activities discussed in previous chapters.

Do:
- Dress professionally.
- Shake the interviewer's hand. Maintain strong eye contact.
- Know about the school you are interviewing for.
- Have your top three selling points in the back of your mind to weave into the conversation.
- Use stories or examples when possible to further your response.

- Be personable and relatable.
- Ask for clarity if you're not familiar with the terminology being used.
- Have questions ready when the interviewer allows for your questions at the end of the interview.

Don't:
- Talk for too long in any one response.
- Pretend that you have all of the answers to education.
- Be late. (If you can't be on time, be early!)
- Have anything on social media that is going to be deemed unprofessional or raise a red flag.
- Talk poorly about a former principal or colleague.

We shouldn't be waiting until college, though, to practice job interview skills. In our time as principals, we have both interviewed many candidates who were grossly underprepared for their interview. That doesn't mean they weren't qualified for the job or that they would not have done well in the position, but you only get one chance to make a first impression. And when a principal, manager, CEO, human resources officer, or hiring agent has back-to-back-to-back interviews, you've got to bring your A game!

Preparing students for these life skills is not as challenging as it sounds, but it does require intentionality. Even as early as elementary school, parents and teachers can practice asking children questions and working on how they respond.

One trick to teach is the technique of buying thinking time by restating the question. When someone asks a difficult or unexpected question during an interview, it might be hard to come up with a great response off the cuff. By restating the question, interviewees buy an extra second or two to compose their thinking and come up with a thoughtful response. For example, the question is, "What would you do if a child told you that he was not eating dinner at night and he is hungry?" Instead of simply saying, "I would . . . ", you could start with "If a child told me they were not eating at night and is hungry, I would . . ." Simply restating that question bought me about two additional seconds to formulate an answer.

Teaching and encouraging your children to use the SPECIAL techniques discussed in chapter 2 will help build confidence in responding to people when they are asked a question. In our experience, this training can start as young as age four. Can you imagine the difference in a child's future, no matter his or her circumstances, if social skills were being learned at such an early age?

INTERNSHIPS

In addition to working with students on skills like résumé writing and interviewing, providing opportunities to build professional capacity on a regular basis will make jobs and careers seem more realistic and attainable. We must move away from the mindset that certain jobs or careers are only for certain types of people. To do this, it is essential that we expose students at an early age to a wide range of jobs and careers performed by people of every color and gender. Classrooms and schools can help provide real-world leadership training that assists students in recognizing future opportunities. When we are able to offer all students these opportunities, not just those born with societal privilege, we will begin to close the social-class achievement gap.

When it comes to preparing students for future jobs and careers, perhaps no school system has done it better than the Cristo Rey Network. Cristo Rey is a nationwide system of high schools that "integrates four years of rigorous college preparatory academics with four years of professional work experience through the Corporate Work Study Program."

Serving inner-city youth coming from mostly limited economic backgrounds, this innovative approach places students in four-year internships with businesses in the local community while still allowing for the completion of all high school requirements. In return for students' work, businesses and corporations fund most of the students' school tuition. They've boasted a 90 percent college enrollment rate during their twenty-year existence and now have alumni working in law, business, finance, and more.[6]

While this unique model may not work everywhere, the foundation is transferable: expose students to real-life jobs at an early age to learn skills, build interests, and network within the workplace. Recall Todd's social media intern program. Social media jobs are sprouting up rapidly in businesses, and early training can provide students with a feel for how the job works. As students reach legal working age, local businesses that can find ways to offer internships are building an infrastructure for their own future by investing in bright minds who may eventually return to work for them.

ADAM

At Moore Elementary, there was a program for deaf and hard-of-hearing students. Most of the students were mainstreamed for part or all of the day, so their classmates were exposed to sign language through an interpreter in the room. One of my students, Keeleigh, had a deaf girl in her kindergarten class and immediately wanted to learn to sign. Over the years, she watched YouTube videos and found books to teach herself the language. By her fifth grade year, she told me that she wanted to be an interpreter, so we arranged for her to help our school interpreters with the younger students. Keeleigh also helped in the office and could communicate with our deaf parents when they came into the building. It was important to me and our interpreters to make sure that her passion for sign language and the hard work she had put in could be seen as a future career. These opportunities gave Keeleigh exactly that.

---

6 See cristoreynetwork.org for more details.

CONCLUSION

As educators, we have to help grow every part of our children and to prepare them to be their most successful selves. This begins with the leadership training that we discussed in the beginning of the book. Keeping the end in mind with experiences such as mock interviews, résumé writing, and internships, we can then work backward to ensure that we are overtly teaching the required pieces that lead to a better end.

To have a successful mock interview, students should be versed on how to offer a firm handshake, have strong eye contact, and proper listening and speaking posture. To take on an internship, students should be aware of the responsibilities that go into a job and the consequences that can come if they do not perform to the best of their ability. And even when students hit a bump in the road and things aren't going their way, having a firm foundation of leadership character and experience will allow them to pick themselves up much quicker than if they did not have them. All these competencies are built in the earliest stages of leadership development.

The leadership character they are building from an early age will culminate in these greater experiences when adults pave a path that spirals around and supports each subsequent layer. This is why it is vital for adults to have open communication, consistent practices, and a common mission when training and developing young leaders. The schools and districts that maintain an eye on the prize (cultivating well-rounded citizens) design and execute the most impactful leadership training systems and outcomes.

LEADERS' REFLECTION QUESTIONS:

1. Were you afforded privileges or opportunities growing up that allowed you to experience or witness what it takes to be prepared for a job or career?
2. How do you include career readiness in the instruction at your school? What intentional lessons are being taught so that students are more prepared for their future (particularly if it is not modeled at home)?

> Share on social media examples of ways you are preparing students for the real world at your school. Use the hashtag #WhenKidsLead.

CONCLUSION

CELEBRATING LEADERSHIP

*A leader is someone you can follow and trust. A
leader is someone that understands what you say
and will work with you to help you.*

—COY, AGE 9

There's nothing wrong with celebrating a job well done. Look all
around, people are always being recognized for their efforts. We
watch award shows that honor athletes, actors, singers, scientists,
writers, and so on. Biographies are written and movies are made
about people who have made a positive impact on the world. In some
cases, people even earn additional money or gifts by working hard
or meeting goals. Recognizing others for their talents and efforts is
a way to let them know that they are appreciated. It's also something
great leaders do.

Being on the receiving end of recognition can be tremendously
rewarding for some and terrifying for others. People react differently

to being acknowledged, and as adults, we need to be cognizant of how our children and students react to that praise.

There are students who relish the spotlight and soak up compliments and recognition like a sponge. Some will even go so far as to do kind or helpful things with the intent of being recognized.

ADAM

Early in my teaching career, I had a fifth-grade student who I once caught placing a candy wrapper on the floor, and then waiting for the moment when she could see I was watching her so she could pick up the wrapper and throw it away. I responded, "I appreciate your throwing the garbage away, but next time you don't need to put it on the floor first."

Then you will have students who shudder at the thought of being recognized for doing something positive. Clapping for them or bringing them up to be recognized in front of others is scary and embarrassing to them. They don't mind being told "good job," but that's as far as they want the recognition to go.

As principals, we both created ways to recognize students for showing leadership. We realized that not every student wants to be recognized on a grand scale, so we created various systems in our schools that allowed us to celebrate very simply or in a big way.

AWESOME OFFICE VISITS

Fill in this sentence:

_____ kids get sent to the principal's office.

If you filled in the blank with a word like *bad* or *trouble* than you probably grew up like many of us. The perception of the principal's office hasn't changed much from generation to generation. What if we were to rethink that perception? Can you imagine going to the principal's office when you were caught being good?

ADAM

When I became a principal, tackling this age-old issue became one of my goals.

On my first day on the job, I walked into my new office and found a stack of folders on top of a round table in the corner of the room. Inside the folders were budgets to be completed, hiring that needed to be done, handbooks that needed updating, and other work that needed to be addressed before the school year started.

I am a checklist kind of person. I function best when I have a list of things on a sticky note that I can check off as I complete them. I've even been known to do a task that wasn't on the sticky note and write it in only so I can check it off. Anyone else?

Well, as I looked at this pile of folders in front of me—with no sticky note—I became overwhelmed. I panicked because there was so much to get done and I didn't know where to start. I said to myself, "I'm done before I ever started." After a little deep breathing, I resolved that if I was going to do this, I had to be able to accomplish just one thing first.

So I hopped in my car and took a trip down the street to Home Depot to buy a can of black chalkboard paint, some rollers, paintbrushes, and drop cloths. When I returned, my wife and I transformed a large white wall in my office into a giant chalkboard. This wall not only became my first checklist item to check off but also symbolized an important step in what I wanted to create in my office: a place where students would be celebrated.

When I met with my new staff in our opening meeting, I introduced what I called Awesome Office Visits, a system where any adult in the building—teachers, office staff, custodians, cafeteria workers, and so on—could recognize a student for something positive. The reasons could include academic achievement, consistent positive character, tremendous growth in an area, a single great feat, or anything else that the adult deemed worthy of this honor.

I provided the staff with a golden-colored form that allowed the adults to fill out the student's name, homeroom teacher, why they were receiving the visit, and a signature. After receiving the form, the student would come down to the office. Upon coming into the main office, the secretaries in the front office would clap for the student and then send the student back to my office.

A'lani writing her name on the Awesome Office Visit wall.

Adam's son Ryder receiving an Awesome Office Visit
for excelling as a classroom greeter.

When these students came into my office, I would congratulate them on the achievement and talk to them about how they earned the recognition. They would get a piece of chalk from a bucket and sign my chalkboard wall. Then I would ask them for their phone number, but only about a quarter of them ever knew what it was, so I would look it up on my student information site. We would call whoever they wanted to call to let them know about the Awesome Visit.

When we called their parent, grandparent, or guardian, the phone call could go one of two ways:

1. If this was a student who never got in trouble and always did their best in school, the person answering the phone would see the school phone number pop up on their phone and answer in a panic. "Are they okay?" and "Did they get hurt?" were the typical responses to our call.

2. If this was a student who may have had previous run-ins with not following the rules and a phone call from the school was typically something negative, the person answering the phone would answer, "What did they do now?"

In either scenario, it was always a relief when I was able to inform the person that this was for a great reason! Over time, our families learned that a phone call from school can be a good thing.

For me, it was so refreshing hearing the excitement from parents as I made these calls. I had parents in tears on the phone, especially from those families that were used to receiving bad news. I also had parents offering up rewards for their child upon getting the recognition—dinner out, new video games, and even a reduced punishment that they had earned at home! I could be having the worst day, and just one positive phone call home could switch it up after hearing the joy from the parents on the other end.

There were also students who requested not to call home. They either didn't feel like being celebrated that way or they wanted to make it a surprise for when they got home. I respected those choices as well, and we kept the congratulations to just putting their name on the wall.

I still remember the very first Awesome Office Visit I ever had. It was a fourth grader named Mark. Unfortunately, Mark was no stranger to the office in the years previous to my arrival. He had struggled immensely in third grade and was frequently getting in trouble for messing around and fighting. His fourth-grade teacher, who rightfully started him off with a clean slate to start the year, saw how hard he was working on his behavior. He was even becoming a role model for others.

He sent him down to the office with the first-ever Awesome Office Visit, and I'll never forget the smile on his face. Mark was so proud of this accomplishment. When I called his mom, I remember her saying to him, "Doesn't this feel good?" I could see Mark light up when she said that, and you could tell it did feel good. He continued to make good choices and even received another Awesome Office Visit later in the year!

These days, many administrators have joined in on making these positive phone calls and have created their own versions of the visit. I have also been excited to see teachers creating their own version of the awesome wall inside their classrooms. Whether it's chalkboard paint, a dry erase board, or even a piece of butcher paper, the act of recognizing students for their hard work and making positive phone calls home go a long way in building leadership traits within our students and reinforcing the behaviors we want to see from them.

HATS-OFF CARDS

TODD

I've always said that I would never be the leader who had a treasure box in the office. I don't want kids doing what's expected because they know they'll get a prize. Plus, when we give tangible prizes, we always have to one-up ourselves, and that gets expensive! I want kids to do well because it feels good to do good. And those positive phone calls home have done just that. Our kids who end up making poor choices most often are also the ones we find ways to send the most hats-off cards to, because as they are learning to control their impulses and make better choices, we want to continually remind them (and their families) we also see the goodness inside.

There was one student in particular whose phone call will forever stick with me. He was a student who often was considered a discipline issue. In addition to his frequent outbursts, he also struggled quite a bit academically. The combination often resulted in him being reprimanded or left with negative consequences.

One day, he came running into my office waving his hats-off card. He was over-the-moon excited that he had worked incredibly hard to earn a celebratory phone call home. I remember putting my office phone on speaker and dialing his mother's number. When she answered, I excitedly told her that her son had earned a hats-off card and that we were so incredibly proud of him and his hard work. I wasn't expecting what came next. The mother replied, "Are you kidding me? You called me on my cell phone to tell me that? What a joke. Tell him to go back to class."

I was floored. I had never had a parent have any reaction other than joy. I watched as the little boy before me, who had run into my office filled with pride, crumpled under his mother's words. As I noticed his eyes beginning to well with tears, I pulled him close to me, looked straight into his eyes, and told him that even though our family may not always act proud of us, he had a principal and a teacher who couldn't be more proud of the young man he was working to become, and that the next time he got a hats-off card we would celebrate it even bigger.

I told him I was proud of him, that I loved him, and that I couldn't wait to see the next great thing he was going to do!

Though those words couldn't take away his pain completely, I hoped they would at least provide him with some comfort. And you know what? That month, he earned three more hats-off cards. And when I brought him in to celebrate and asked him who he wanted to share the good news with, he didn't choose his mom. Instead he chose the school nurse and the music teacher, and then he asked me if I would have lunch with him instead of calling home. Sometimes a child wants our time as much as our celebration.

This entire experience was also a reminder to me of what our kids are often coming from at home. When kids act out, misbehave, or make poor choices, we are often so quick to jump straight to consequences instead of first seeking to understand the underlying issues.

EVERYONE DESERVES HATS OFF

I always say that adults are just big kids. The only difference is adults end up crying way more than children. When I started seeing the powerful impact that hats-off cards were having on our students and their families, I knew I had to continue that with the adults. And though this book may be entitled *When Kids Lead,* it's important to remember the example we set for our children because they're always watching, even when we don't notice.

I still remember the first hats-off card I wrote to a staff member. It was for my assistant principal, Aaron Marvel. To build a little suspense, I had asked him to meet me in my office at the end of the day. We all think we're in trouble when the principal asks to meet with us in the office at the end of the day.

As he walked into my office that afternoon, I smiled and held up a hats-off card. I let him know that I had written one for him because of the great work he did in organizing our testing materials. As I saw the smile creep across his face, I could see he wasn't quite prepared for my next question: "Now who do you want me to call?" At first he assumed I was joking, but as I quickly informed him of my seriousness, he answered, "Um, I guess my mom?"

As the phone rang on speaker and his mom answered, I quickly informed her who I was and why I was calling. I let her know that I was the principal where her son worked and that he was in my office, but not to worry because he wasn't in trouble! I then thanked her for the fantastic work she did in raising her son, and I thanked her for sharing him with us, and I let her know what a great job he did with organizing our testing materials. My favorite part of the call? Her response of "Aw, my baby, Aaron!" and seeing the wave of red wash across Aaron's face.

Even though it was incredibly special in the moment, a conversation with Aaron about a week later really helped me see the power of that moment. Aaron came into my office to let me know that making that phone call was probably one of the coolest moments of his adult life so far. Why? Because as children, our parents hopefully hear great stuff about us all the time. But how many times as adults will our boss call home to our family to celebrate the great work we're doing? That's true especially when our family isn't filled with educators who understand the amount of heart and energy we pour into our jobs every day.

Those five minutes of my time, which didn't cost me any money, made more of an impact than any amount of school-branded items I could have gifted Aaron. Those are the moments as leaders that we can heap upon everyone around us. And the more goodness we spread, the more we impact, and the better our world becomes.

THE MAGIC GATE

ADAM

Each week at Moore Magnet, I conducted a ceremony with the whole school where five students were recognized for being amazing scholars and friends. Each of the five students came from one of the five houses (a la Harry Potter) that we had at our school.[7] An adult from each house would come to the front of the gym and announce in front of the entire school which student from their house would have the honor of spinning the game wheel that we had constructed. With the wheel, spinners were able to earn extra points for their house.

After the ceremony was over and the rest of the school had gone back to their classrooms, my assistant principal and I took the five students to the front lobby of the school, where on the wall hung a large painted gate, beautifully refurbished and designed by my art teacher, Teresa Wiles. On the front of the gate was a lock, and inside the gate was a silver metallic bag.

In the hand I held out in front of the five students were five identical-looking keys, which were inspired by Unlock the Magic, a reward my friend Hope King had done with her class. Each student selected one key, and I informed them that only one would open the lock. I also reminded them that the other four do not but that each of them should be proud because they were selected by their house that day to represent the team, and that was a huge honor in itself.

I always let the youngest of the students present go first, and then we went up in age from there. Once we had discovered the student with the special key, we opened up the gate and that student

---

7 We encourage you to check out the work of the Ron Clark Academy to learn more about houses and how you can build your own system at your school.

looked inside the magic silver metallic bag. And inside the bag was ... a bunch of random dollar-store items. Normally, this would not elicit much of a response from a child, because frankly there wasn't anything all that special in there. But the fact that this ceremony was built up to be such an honor, you would have thought the child just won the lottery.

Trying to unlock the Magic Gate!

I had students running back to class to show their classmates the slinky that they had just chosen from the magic gate. I had others cheering and crying because they got a new deck of cards or silly putty. This reaffirmed for me that it is not about what you have but rather what you make of it.

As we take small moments to recognize students for their accomplishments in any number of ways, remind yourself that this is *their* moment and we need to make it as special as we can. When adults put excitement, energy, and a little bit of anticipation and mystery into recognizing students, it makes it even more special for the children on the receiving end.

When growing our kids into leaders we need to let them see the power of a kind word. They need to experience how it makes them feel. They can't just be told. The more we can help our kids see the importance of building others up and celebrating the success of others, the more we're helping them grow into leaders any of us would be honored to follow.

CONCLUSION

When we set out to write this book, we wanted to create something that any adult could use as a starting point to understand the importance of growing student leaders by offering concrete examples and strategies.

We are by no means experts in this area, but it is an area that we are extremely passionate about. We have seen time and time again the importance of empowering kids, inspiring them to find their voice, and growing them in their possibilities.

We hope this book has inspired you to take a few steps outside of your comfort zone and try something new. The biggest changes in history started by someone deciding they weren't happy with the status quo.

Will you make mistakes? Of course. Will you have people tell you your ideas are crazy? Heck, yeah. But we'd rather be called crazy and do what we know is best for kids than to have sat back in our own fears and insecurities wondering, What if . . .?

So get out there, challenge the norms, do the unexpected, and be a champion for our kids. You'll see incredible things happen when you get out of the way and let kids lead.

LEADERS' REFLECTION QUESTIONS:

1. Do you have a childhood memory of winning a reward or being recognized for something great that you did? How did it make you feel? Did that encourage you to continue that positive behavior?

2. What currently exists in your school or classroom to recognize leaders for their accomplishments? Are all types of achievements recognized, or only the traditional things such as honor roll and attendance?

Share on social media how your students are recognized at school and at home for being leaders. Use the hashtag #WhenKidsLead.

APPENDIX

BOOKS THAT CULTIVATE LEADERSHIP

Here are a few (but by no means all) of the diverse books that we highly recommend adding to any classroom or school library. We don't believe in blanket lists that identify the grade level appropriateness of books, so as you peruse the list below, please make sure you look up the content of each book to ensure you find it appropriate for the ages of the children you want to introduce it to.

PICTURE BOOKS:

- *A Boy Like You* by Frank Murphy
- *The Proudest Blue* by Ibtihaj Muhammad
- *Mommy's Khimar* by Jamilah Thompkins-Bigelow
- *Red* by Michael Hall
- *Chocolate Milk, Por Favor* by Maria Dismondy
- *Bilal Cooks Daal* by Aisha Saeed
- *Benji, The Bad Day, and Me* by Sally Pla
- *Be Kind* by Pat Zietlow Miller
- *When Grandma Gives You a Lemon Tree* by Jamie Dennihan
- *Most People* by Michael Leannah

- *Write to Me* by Cynthia Grady
- *Say Something* by Peter H. Reynolds
- *Knock: My Dad's Dream for Me* by Daniel Beaty
- *Ada Twist, Scientist* by Andrea Beaty
- *The Night Dad Went to Jail* by Melissa Higgins
- *Love* by Matt de la Pena
- *The Last Stop on Market Street* by Matt de la Pena
- *Sulwe* by Lupita Nyong'o
- *Grumpy Monkey* by Suzanne Lang
- *The Invisible Boy* by Trudy Ludwig
- *I Want to be A Lot* by Ashley Savage
- *Douglas You Need Glasses* by Ged Adamson
- *And That's Why She's My Mama* by Tiarra Nazario
- *Sticks* by Diane Alber
- *Festival of Colors* by Surishtha Sehgal
- *Fry Bread* by Kevin Noble Maillard
- *I Will Be Fierce* by Bea Birdsong
- *Under My Hijab* by Hena Khan
- *The Cool Bean* by Jory John and Pete Oswald
- *The Wild Card Kids* by Hope and Wade King
- *Spruce and Lucy* by Todd Nesloney

CHAPTER BOOKS/GRAPHIC NOVELS:

- *Ghost Boys* by Jewell Parker Rhodes
- *The Boy at the Back of the Class* by Onjali Q. Raúf
- *Internment* by Samira Ahmed
- *Hey Kiddo* by Jarrett Krosoczka
- *New Kid* by Jerry Craft
- *Insignificant Events in the Life of a Cactus* by Dusti Bowling
- *Momentous Events in the Life of a Cactus* by Dusti Bowling (fantastic sequel)
- *Someday Birds* by Sally Pla

- *Stanley Will Probably Be Fine* by Sally Pla
- *Front Desk* by Kelly Yang
- *Orbiting Jupiter* by Gary D. Schmidt
- *Children of Blood and Bone* by Tomi Adeyemi
- *Allegedly* by Tiffany D. Jackson
- *On the Come Up* by Angie Thomas
- *Train I Ride* by Paul Mosier
- *Look Both Ways: A Tale Told In Ten Blocks* by Jason Reynolds
- *Clean Getaway* by Nic Stone
- *Wishtree* by Katherine Applegate
- *Song for a Whale* by Lynne Kelly
- *Far from the Tree* by Robin Benway
- *The Bridge Home* by Padma Venkatraman
- *The 57 Bus* by Dashka Slater
- *I'm Not Your Perfect Mexican Daughter* by Erika L. Sanchez
- *The Gauntlet* by Karuna Riazi
- *Braced* by Allyson Gerber
- *Pashmina* by Nidhi Chanani
- *The Serpent's Secret* by Sayantani DasGupta
- *Lucky Broken Girl* by Ruth Behar
- *Ban This Book* by Alan Gratz
- *Refugee* by Alan Gratz
- *Rebound* by Kwame Alexander
- *Lions and Liars* by Kate Beasley
- *You Go First* by Erin Entrada Kelly
- *The Serpent King* by Jeff Zentner
- *Two Can Keep a Secret* by Karen McManus
- *Words on Bathroom Walls* by Julia Walton

ACKNOWLEDGMENTS

ADAM

To my wife, Jaclyn: Thank you for the support and encouragement to continue to reach for my dreams and take the paths that are presented.

To my mom, my dad, and Marc: Thank you for cultivating my leadership since I was young. I would have never been what I am today without you all.

To Moore Magnet Elementary: You gave me a chance and I will never forget that. Thank you to the staff, students, and families who embraced crazy suits and raising the bar for what a school can be.

TODD

To my wife, Lissette: Thank you for always jumping on board with my crazy ideas, for the travels, experiences, laughs, and dreams. I couldn't do this journey without you.

To Webb Elementary: Many of these ideas were born out of collaboration with my former school family. I am so thankful for the years we had together and look forward to following your many new endeavours in always doing what's best for kids!

To friends: You know who you are without having to have me list your names. I couldn't have made it through the past few years without you all. Your words of encouragement, support, challenges, and so much more have made me the man I am today.

FROM BOTH OF US

To Dave and Shelley: Thank you for believing in us for this book! You have both changed the landscape of publishing and we are all so appreciative of what you do.

To Marisol: We appreciate your honesty and critical eye. This book is so much better because of you.

To Sal and the Reading List: It was a pleasure working with each of you in this process. The immense time and knowledge you offered us is greatly appreciated. Thank you for making this book a reality!

To Katie, Hope, and Jose: Your creative and artistic minds are invaluable! Thank you for your feedback and friendship!

To the Get Your Teach On Team: Thank you all for your friendship, support, and magic making! Hope and Wade, thank you for trusting us to create Get Your Lead On to inspire school leaders from across the country!

To the reader: Thank you for supporting our dream and buying this book. We hope it encourages and inspires you to push forward!

ABOUT THE AUTHORS

ADAM DOVICO

Adam Dovico is an accomplished teacher, principal, author, speaker, and professor. He began his career in North Carolina as an elementary school teacher then worked as a teacher and the school implementation specialist for the renowned Ron Clark Academy, where he traveled across the country conducting professional development and on-site training for schools. Adam returned to his alma mater, Wake Forest University, to train the next generation of teachers as a clinical professor. Most recently, he's served as the principal at Moore Magnet Elementary. Adam is married to Jaclyn Dovico, and they have two sons, Ryder and Maddox.

You can follow Adam on social media @adamdovico and visit his website at adamdovico.com.

TODD NESLONEY

Todd Nesloney is the director of culture and strategic leadership for the Texas Elementary Principals and Supervisors Association (TEPSA). He was previously a principal / lead learner at a pre-K–5 school in Texas. He is an award-winning author for his work on *Kids Deserve It!* and *Sparks in the Dark*. He has also written the book *Stories from Webb* and self-published a children's book, *Spruce & Lucy*. Todd has been recognized by John C. Maxwell as a Top 10 Finalist for the 2018 Transformational Leadership Award, by the

White House and President Barack Obama as a Connected Educator "Champion of Change," the National School Board Association as one of the 20 to Watch in Education, the Center for Digital Education as one of their Top 40 Innovators in Education, the BAMMYs as the National Elementary Principal of the Year and the National Elementary Teacher of the Year, and the Texas Computer Education Association as their Texas Elementary Teacher of the Year.

Todd is also a two-time TEDx speaker. He travels and speaks about his innovative practices and how we have to stop making excuses for why we can't do things for our students. Todd also speaks about his use of technology in the classroom and with his school and gives educators ideas on how to continually utilize the tools at our disposal to create the best possible learning environments for children. He currently hosts the podcast series *Tell Your Story* and actively blogs and share his stories through many different social media venues. He is married to Lissette Nesloney, and they live in a small community in Brenham, Texas.

You can follow Todd on social media @TechNinjaTodd and visit his website at toddnesloney.com.

Bring Todd and Adam to Your Organization or Event!
Contact Ryan at ryan@premierespeakers.com for booking.

MORE FROM

Dave Burgess Consulting, Inc.

Since 2012, DBCI has been publishing books that inspire and equip educators to be their best. For more information on our titles or to purchase bulk orders for your school, district, or book study, visit **DaveBurgessconsulting.com/DBCIbooks.**

MORE LEADERSHIP & SCHOOL CULTURE

Culturize by Jimmy Casas

Escaping the School Leader's Dunk Tank by Rebecca Coda and Rick Jetter

From Teacher to Leader by Starr Sackstein

The Innovator's Mindset by George Couros

It's OK to Say "They" by Christy Whittlesey

Kids Deserve It! by Todd Nesloney and Adam Welcome

Live Your Excellence by Jimmy Casas

Let Them Speak by Rebecca Coda and Rick Jetter

The Limitless School by Abe Hege and Adam Dovico

Next-Level Teaching by Jonathan Alsheimer

The Pepper Effect by Sean Gaillard

The Principled Principal by Jeffrey Zoul and Anthony McConnell

Relentless by Hamish Brewer

The Secret Solution by Todd Whitaker, Sam Miller, and Ryan Donlan

Start. Right. Now. by Todd Whitaker, Jeffrey Zoul, and Jimmy Casas

Stop. Right. Now. by Jimmy Casas and Jeffrey Zoul

Teach Your Class Off by CJ Reynolds

They Call Me "Mr. De" by Frank DeAngelis

Unmapped Potential by Julie Hasson and Missy Lennard

Word Shift by Joy Kirr

Your School Rocks by Ryan McLane and Eric Lowe

LIKE A PIRATE™ SERIES

Teach Like a PIRATE by Dave Burgess

eXPlore Like a Pirate by Michael Matera

Learn Like a Pirate by Paul Solarz

Play Like a Pirate by Quinn Rollins

Run Like a Pirate by Adam Welcome

LEAD LIKE A PIRATE™ SERIES

Lead Like a PIRATE by Shelley Burgess and Beth Houf

Balance Like a Pirate by Jessica Cabeen, Jessica Johnson, and
     Sarah Johnson

Lead beyond Your Title by Nili Bartley

Lead with Appreciation by Amber Teamann and Melinda Miller

Lead with Culture by Jay Billy

Lead with Instructional Rounds by Vicki Wilson

Lead with Literacy by Mandy Ellis

TECHNOLOGY & TOOLS

50 Things You Can Do with Google Classroom by Alice Keeler and
     Libbi Miller

50 Things to Go Further with Google Classroom by Alice Keeler and
     Libbi Miller

140 Twitter Tips for Educators by Brad Currie, Billy Krakower, and
     Scott Rocco

Block Breaker by Brian Aspinall

Code Breaker by Brian Aspinall

Google Apps for Littles by Christine Pinto and Alice Keeler

Master the Media by Julie Smith

Reality Bytes by Christine Lion-Bailey, Jesse Lubinsky, and
     Micah Shippee, PhD

Shake Up Learning by Kasey Bell

Social LEADia by Jennifer Casa-Todd

Stepping up to Google Classroom by Alice Keeler and Kimberly Mattina

Teaching Math with Google Apps by Alice Keeler and Diana Herrington

Teachingland by Amanda Fox and Mary Ellen Weeks

TEACHING METHODS & MATERIALS

All 4s and 5s by Andrew Sharos

Boredom Busters by Katie Powell

The Classroom Chef by John Stevens and Matt Vaudrey

The Collaborative Classroom by Trevor Muir

Copyrighteous by Diana Gill

Ditch That Homework by Matt Miller and Alice Keeler

Ditch That Textbook by Matt Miller

Don't Ditch That Tech by Matt Miller, Nate Ridgway, and Angelia Ridgway

EDrenaline Rush by John Meehan

Educated by Design by Michael Cohen, The Tech Rabbi

The EduProtocol Field Guide by Marlena Hebern and Jon Corippo

The EduProtocol Field Guide: Book 2 by Marlena Hebern and Jon Corippo

Instant Relevance by Denis Sheeran

LAUNCH by John Spencer and A.J. Juliani

Make Learning MAGICAL by Tisha Richmond

Pure Genius by Don Wettrick

The Revolution by Darren Ellwein and Derek McCoy

Shift This! by Joy Kirr

Skyrocket Your Teacher Coaching by Michael Cary Sonbert

Spark Learning by Ramsey Musallam

Sparks in the Dark by Travis Crowder and Todd Nesloney

Table Talk Math by John Stevens

The Wild Card by Hope and Wade King

The Writing on the Classroom Wall by Steve Wyborney

INSPIRATION, PROFESSIONAL GROWTH & PERSONAL DEVELOPMENT

Be REAL by Tara Martin

Be the One for Kids by Ryan Sheehy

The Coach ADVenture by Amy Illingworth

Creatively Productive by Lisa Johnson

Educational Eye Exam by Alicia Ray

The EduNinja Mindset by Jennifer Burdis

Empower Our Girls by Lynmara Colón and Adam Welcome

Finding Lifelines by Andrew Grieve and Andrew Sharos

The Four O'Clock Faculty by Rich Czyz

How Much Water Do We Have? by Pete and Kris Nunweiler

P Is for Pirate by Dave and Shelley Burgess

A Passion for Kindness by Tamara Letter

The Path to Serendipity by Allyson Apsey

Sanctuaries by Dan Tricarico

The SECRET SAUCE by Rich Czyz

Shattering the Perfect Teacher Myth by Aaron Hogan

Stories from Webb by Todd Nesloney

Talk to Me by Kim Bearden

Teach Better by Chad Ostrowski, Tiffany Ott, Rae Hughart, and Jeff Gargas

Teach Me, Teacher by Jacob Chastain

Teach, Play, Learn! by Adam Peterson

TeamMakers by Laura Robb and Evan Robb

Through the Lens of Serendipity by Allyson Apsey

The Zen Teacher by Dan Tricarico

CHILDREN'S BOOKS

Beyond Us by Aaron Polansky

Cannonball In by Tara Martin

Dolphins in Trees by Aaron Polansky

I Want to Be a Lot by Ashley Savage

The Princes of Serendip by Allyson Apsey

The Wild Card Kids by Hope and Wade King

Zom-Be a Design Thinker by Amanda Fox

Made in the USA
Las Vegas, NV
21 March 2021